# Creative Journaling for Teachers

## A Visual Approach to

 Declutter Thoughts

 Manage Time

 Boost Productivity

 Nichole Carter

**INTERNATIONAL SOCIETY FOR TECHNOLOGY IN EDUCATION**
**PORTLAND, OREGON • ARLINGTON, VIRGINIA**

# Creative Journaling for Teachers
## A Visual Approach to Declutter Thoughts, Manage Time and Boost Productivity
Nichole Carter

Acquisitions Editor: *Valerie Witte*

Editor: *Emily Reed*

Copy Editor: *Joanna Szabo*

Proofreader: *Laura Gibson*

Indexer: *Kento Ikeda*

Book Design and Production: *Danielle Foster*

Cover Design: *Christina DeYoung*


Library of Congress Cataloging-in-Publication Data

Names: Carter, Nichole, author.

Title: Creative journaling for teachers : a visual approach to declutter
  thoughts, manage time and boost productivity / Nichole Carter.

Identifiers: LCCN 2022004095 | ISBN 9781564849526 (paperback) | ISBN
  9781564849533 (epub) | ISBN 9781564849540 (pdf)

Subjects: LCSH: Reflective teaching. | Lesson planning. | Teachers—Time
  management. | Teachers—Job stress. | Teachers—Mental health.

Classification: LCC LB1025.3 .C38634 2022 | DDC 371.14/4—dc23/eng/20220302

LC record available at https://lccn.loc.gov/2022004095


First Edition

ISBN: 978-1-56484-952-6

Ebook version available


Printed in the United States of America

ISTE® is a registered trademark of the International Society for Technology in Education.

# About ISTE

The International Society for Technology in Education (ISTE) is home to a passionate community of global educators who believe in the power of technology to transform teaching and learning, accelerate innovation and solve tough problems in education.

ISTE inspires the creation of solutions and connections that improve opportunities for all learners by delivering: practical guidance, evidence-based professional learning, virtual networks, thought-provoking events and the ISTE Standards. ISTE is also the leading publisher of books focused on technology in education. For more information or to become an ISTE member, visit iste.org. Subscribe to ISTE's YouTube channel and connect with ISTE on Twitter, Facebook and LinkedIn.

## Related ISTE Titles

*Sketchnoting in the Classroom: A Practical Guide to Deepen Student Learning* by Nichole Carter (2019)

*Stretch Yourself: A Personalized Journey to Deepen Your Teaching Practice* by Caitlin McLemore and Fanny Passeport (2019)

To see all books available from ISTE, please visit **iste.org/books**.

# About the Author

**Nichole Carter** (@MrsCarterHLA) has been in education since 2004. She has taught everything from geography to US history to reading intervention to middle school language arts. After teaching language arts with a ton of tech integration, Nichole changed districts and has been working at the district level, a teacher on special assignment, as a part of a digital curriculum team working with educators from PK to 12th grade on all things instructionally innovative.

In 2016, Nichole decided to start looking into journaling. It was coming up all over social media from Instagram to Pinterest; at the same time, she had been working on learning the ropes of sketchnoting for almost a year. Nichole quickly saw her skills develop in both areas and saw a lot of overlap between drawing containers and using color coding to build hierarchy. In a few short months Nichole led a room of one hundred educators through some of the very basics of the concept of bullet journaling®, especially how it could be harnessed by teachers. She quickly began putting together activities and sessions for both teachers and students to help guide them through some of the basic concepts to see if it was a good fit for them. More than twelve very full journals later, Nichole sees no end in sight; this style of journaling has helped her manifest goals and organize her life.

Professionally and personally, Nichole believes in the power of creating, whether it is in sketchnotes, journaling, art, videos, or even a great plate of pasta. Inspiring other people to create and make is a big part of her educational pedagogy.

Nichole lives with her daughter Molly and her Wheaten Terrier Stewart just outside of Portland, Oregon. With the addition of a much sought after motorhome, named Hannah, Molly and Nichole love to road trip and see the country. She loves to read (meeting her Goodreads goal of at least 160 books a year for the last four years and counting) as well as listen to music, cook, and create art.

## Dedication

To my parents for their unwavering support, and to my daughter: May you find balance in your life to be your happiest self. Thank you for being there for me when life gets dark.

"THE GOAL IS NOT TO BE BETTER THAN THE OTHER MAN, BUT YOUR PREVIOUS SELF."

—THE DALAI LAMA

# Contents

CHAPTER 1
## How Creativity and Reflection Lead to Productivity

CHAPTER 2

# Goal Setting

CHAPTER 3

# Time Management

# Developing a System That Works for You

CHAPTER 5

# Journaling Strategies for Managing Mental Health

# Introduction

In 2017, as I was teaching myself how to sketchnote, I was asked to speak at a local conference where someone I greatly admired was the keynote speaker. That person was Sunni Brown, author of *The Doodle Revolution* and the person who gave the "Doodlers, unite!" talk via TED-Ed. I knew she was going to be talking about the power of doodling and turning that into sketchnotes to unlock your creativity. At the time, sketchnotes were all I could think about, but I knew I couldn't speak on the same topic as Sunni.

Luckily, I had decided to start a bullet journal® earlier that year, in January. It was something that I was seeing pop up more and more in my social media feeds, and the creativity of it appealed to me. I was already down the doodling path due to sketchnoting, and I had always wanted to be the kind of person that journaled, but I would always start a journal and not see it through. Teachers tend to be planners by nature; this just happened to be a happy confluence. When I start something new like this, I dive in. I consume and learn as much as I can, try it out, and then consume even more.

At the tail end of February, I ended up doing a session at that local conference on bullet journaling®. I noticed at this point that my journaling had gotten better because of my sketchnotes, and my sketchnotes had gotten better because of my bullet journaling®. They were inescapably linked. My brain was now starting to rely on this creative outlet, and it helped me stay in touch with my goals and start something in a journal that I am still continuing to this day. I absolutely love looking at my shelf with twelve well-loved journals staring back at me. I like being able to go back through them and read my entries, see my artwork, and remind myself of goals attained.

We have gone through some challenging times, all of us. I have found a mental outlet that has guided me through some very tough times, and I want to share it with more people. We are living in an age where "hustle" and "grind" are a part of our daily lives, and at the same time, we find ourselves questioning that ideology. Teachers are expected to stay on top of their lengthy to-do lists, while the demands on them are greater than ever. I hope this book can provide some tools that teachers—and, by extension, their students—can use to declutter thoughts, manage time better, and remain focused and productive. I also hope that this book can help improve mental health, as well as lead to better self-awareness and time management.

# What's in This Book

This book focuses on tools for educators to apply in their own practice. However, each chapter will also include sections focused on helping students develop these critical skills so they can become more productive in their work as well. We will begin by looking at how creativity and reflection can help unlock productivity, and then start working on goal setting to bring your own priorities to the forefront. We will then focus on time management and from there, on making the journal fit your own personal needs. One of the benefits of using a system like this is that you don't have to deal with premade layouts and designs that don't work for you. You can personalize to your heart's content. Finally, we will go into specifics around the mental health benefits of journaling. Throughout the book, you will be presented with "try this" moments that will encourage you to write in the book or in your journal, use apps, use provided materials (playlists, editable and printable materials, digital planners etc.), and reflect.

Just like *Sketchnoting in the Classroom*, this book features layouts and examples, calendar ideas, prompts, and more. While focused on journaling, the book explores a whole host of ideas relating to creativity, productivity, and mental health. Ultimately, this is a book meant to inspire you to get started on your own journaling journey.

# Who This Book Is For

This book is for teachers that feel like they could use some ideas on how to prioritize their to-do list and spark some creativity and reflection in their lives. However, seeing the many people around the world that have embraced this style of journaling in the last few years, it can clearly benefit anyone, no matter their role. Many of the tips and ideas could be passed onto students in the classroom as well, especially those in secondary education that are starting to work on their own school and life balance.

As you read, I hope you get out your own journal and try some of the challenges and ideas—and I hope you will join me on Twitter, Instagram, or your social media platform of choice using the hashtag **#TeacherJournaling**. Share your thoughts, questions, ideas, and favorite resources with the community.

Happy journaling,

**Nichole**

@MrsCarterHLA

@Nichole444

# CHAPTER 1

# How Creativity and Reflection Lead to Productivity

## CHAPTER OBJECTIVES

- Understand the concept behind dot journaling and how you can customize the experience to work for your brain
- Participate in a creativity challenge to start your journaling process and get your creative juices flowing
- Know that creativity can lead to satisfaction and productivity
- Be able to identify what your needs are when journaling
- Recognize the importance of taking time for self-reflection (in any form!)
- Have the tools to start building your own journal
- Connect the mindfulness analysis approach to your professional goals
- Know more about cultivating student creativity and how journaling can help

## SUPPLY LIST

- journal with dot grid
- pens
- highlighters
- washi tape or stickers
- magazines or images for collage

## VOCABULARY

- bullet journaling®
- reflective practice
- mindful analysis

One of the biggest realizations I had as I started down my current path was that the more creative I attempted to be, the more creative I was. The coolest thing about being creative and flexing an artistic talent, no matter how small, is that it is something you can keep cultivating. Being creative helps you clear your mind, as well as brainstorm and daydream. Creating space for creativity and daydreaming may help envision goals and support long-term planning.

Journaling isn't always about the end product; it is also about the creative process. This process releases endorphins in our brains, triggering feelings of happiness as well as calming effects. As an adult, it can be incredibly hard to find something that can challenge you, and yet at the same time help you focus, plan, and be creative. For me, finding a way to keep track of my daily tasks, brainstorm both long- and short-term goals, reflect on those goals, and be creative daily came by way of journaling.

You may have heard the terms **bullet journaling**®, dot journaling, or even BuJo; observed others sharing about bullet journaling® online; or seen a dedicated section to blank journals at your local bookstore. At its core, this type of journaling is a way to help our brains filter our thoughts and decisions down into manageable chunks in order to be more productive every day.

As teachers, we have to make thousands of decisions every day. We have to prepare for work before work so that work can happen during work; it's mentally draining. Without a good system to help you stay on top of all the things on your to-do list, important aspects of your work can easily fall to the wayside.

Systems such as planners have been around for ages to help teachers organize and think about the upcoming weeks and months, but what if you could develop your own system, one that morphs to meet your needs? What if you could buy a blank journal and transform it into something that not only keeps track of your to-do list, but also has your calendar and goals and any number of things to help you reflect and be a more creative and productive you? This is where journaling comes in.

Follow the QR code to watch a TED Talk by Ryder Carroll, inventor of the bullet journal® method. After watching the video, ask yourself these questions:

How to Declutter Your Mind—
Keep a Journal

In this TED Talk, Ryder Carroll explains bullet journaling® and how he developed the system to help his ADHD.

- How do you currently declutter your mind? What do you think about asking yourself the questions "is it vital?" and "does it matter?"

- How do you focus on things that interest you and then turn them into actionable goals?

- How often do you give yourself time to reflect?

# How to Get Started Creating, Reflecting, and Planning

A journal with a dot grid (hence the name "dot journaling") and heavyweight paper and a pen is all you need to get started. As you get more comfortable and want to start adding more things to your journaling kit, I would suggest Mildliner dual-tip highlighters and maybe washi tape. The highlighters can add some color to your journal, and the washi tape not only adds some fun, but can also be used to hide mistakes and errors!

The planner industry is a multi-million-dollar industry selling highly specific products to teachers the world over. I can't tell you how many of these planners I have bought over the years and ended up not using, or only

FIGURE 1.1 Some of my journaling supplies. To get started you only need a blank journal and a pen but you will likely discover new tools over time, as I have.

partially using, and then ultimately discarding. I have always been predisposed to wanting to be one of those daily journalers. I would start and stop and start and stop; it was a cycle for me. Bookshelves full of half-completed journals. I think one of the main issues for me is that if I put a planner down and don't use it for a few weeks or months, I get so completely overwhelmed by the "wasted" pages that I have a hard time picking it back up and continuing to use it.

At one point in my educational career, I used a spreadsheet created by a colleague that we would print out in a monthly spread to plan out our curriculum. This was before templates were readily available, and many people in my building used this same box grid monthly layout to help us plan. I also had sticky notes galore all over my desk: anytime I needed a reminder of something that needed to get done, I would write it on a sticky note and plop it somewhere on my teacher desk. No rhyme or real reason.

**Journals to Get Started Blog Post**

In this website post you will find links to several of my favorite journals that range in price, and my thoughts on how they break down compared to each other.

I also went through a phase where I really liked the aesthetic of a Moleskine journal. I started to slip my sticky notes into my journal and take it everywhere with me, again with no organization—that yellow Moleskine journal was a mess.

At one point I started paying for a digital lesson planner service, thinking that if I filled out my lessons really well and had to get a substitute at the last minute, I could just print out those digital lessons and, boom! Sub plans done. It never really worked out that way. And while all of these things centered around my life as a teacher and my daily grind, they lacked a comprehensive system, one that would force me to write down goals, reflect on my personal or professional growth, or track some of my behaviors—both healthy habits and things that I wanted to improve on.

So even now as I reflect on what got me to this point, I realize I was slowly finding my way to this path with a lot of hits and misses. Teachers, I think, are inherently drawn to all the things that make dot journaling fun, creative, and fulfilling. We like structure and planning things out. Most of us like stationery to some extent—especially pens, all kinds of pens!

So find a journal (scan the QR for some suggestions to get started) and let's start journaling together!

# Creativity Leads to Satisfaction and Productivity

Sometimes getting out of our comfort zones and putting our thoughts and ideas onto paper can help them seem more concrete and even help us to define things that we really feel are important. When I sit down to think about the week ahead and prioritize things that need to get done (as well as add a little bit of color and whimsy), my brain has a chance to calm down, my blood pressure lowers, and I have managed to spend a little bit of time away from the screen. I will occasionally use social media for inspiration, or an app to track how I did on a particular habit, but for the most part I have struck a balance between organizing my to-do list, understanding my upcoming meetings and commitments for the week, and putting aside some time for creativity and self-reflection or self-betterment.

Writing can be a great way to clear the mind. I love having a good prompt to help with reflective writing. Prompts can get me to write a full page, or even just little snippets about what has happened over the last month of my life and what needs to be carried over into the new month. Honestly, it isn't about the end result and how it looks. Exactly as I said in my last book, *Sketchnoting in the Classroom*, it isn't about creating art or making something beautiful; it's all about the process. I find that the more chaotic the entries are in my dot journal, the more I love them. It is a peek into my mind.

I love to see my journals on the shelf, banged up and bruised and full of stuff. The writer and artist Austin Kleon once posted an Instagram picture of his journal. He was

### Creativity Playlist

Scanning this QR code will take you to a Spotify playlist that has over a hundred songs and five hours of innovative tracks to spark your creativity and inspiration.

**SATURDAY**
- ☐ Book Research
- ☐ Respond to TOC contents
- ☐ Laundry
- ☐ Caite play date → sleep over

**SUNDAY**
- ☐ Nola Donuts
- ☐ Japanese Garden or Rose Garden
- ☐ Board Games
- ☐ Bujo
- ☐ Pack Serravallo books + Ladies Drawing Night
  - ☐ email Math teachers about deliveries

CREATIVE IS NOT A NOUN

| M | Wipebook, LIT Leaders Prep, iiCadre PD Micheal / Puppy Class |
|---|---|
| T | LIT Leaders |
| W | Prep TIA, BHS Tech Show, TIA meeting, Rockcreek PTC |
| T | Book mtg Sphero Course |
| F | Pep Mtg Day |
| S | OMSI |
| S | OMSI |

**this week:**

Next Week: Week 3 Dog Groomers

**meals:**

| M | Bake Tilapia, Fruit Salad |
|---|---|
| T | Chicken Quesadillas |
| W | Garden Tortellini + Cucumber Salad |
| T | BLT + Garden Salad |
| F | Sausage + Lentils |
| S | |
| S | |

FIGURE 1.2   Here you can see a layout of a typical day or week where I have marked my meetings, my to-do list, and added some fun drawings to fill in the space. Often I will just create the meetings and to-do list portion, and come back later to fill in the space with stickers, washi tape, or doodles.

finishing one journal and starting a new one. The old one was two or three times the size of the new journal. It was filled with extra stuff that had been jammed and glued in, and the pages were worn, full of ink, or warped and discolored. That is what I love about having a physical journal. Seeing it lived in and used up. Kleon mentioned that he weighs his journals at the start and end of using them, to see how much he has physically added to them. I love this concept, having never thought about the physical weight of the things you add to your journal. He has inspired me to start doing that in my journals moving forward.

It's what you pour into your journals that makes them special, in whatever capacity you want. You want less doodling and more to-do lists? Done! You want more reflective journaling and less doodling? Done! You want a hybrid of all of this? Done! Again, the beauty is that you are starting with a blank journal and making it work for you. In the end, if you enjoy doing it and it meets your needs, who cares about what it looks like? When we were children, if we liked something, we went at it with abandon. We just started, without any expectations. Let's take that approach as we move forward.

FIGURE 1.3  Here is an example of a new, unused journal, and one that has been used over a period of time. I love seeing these journals on a bookshelf. Occasionally, I flip back through them. It often isn't the daily to-do tasks that I end up focusing on as I revisit these journals; instead, it's usually the artwork, the creative lists and brain dumps, or reflection writing.

So, I challenge you to just get started. Throw out any expectations and get ready to dive into something where you can add stickers and washi tape and colors and doodles and reflective writing. Choose from one of the following challenges and let's work on finding something that not only fits your needs, but also fills you with joy!

## COLLAGE CREATIVITY CHALLENGE

One of my favorite things to do when I start a new journal, beyond putting my name in it and the start date (and now a starting weight thanks to Austin Kleon), is to create a collage. Making a collage is a great way to unleash creativity and gain a new perspective on things that you like and that are important to you. All you need are scissors, glue, a sheet of paper, and some magazines. Anyone can make a collage. Just start looking for things that speak to you; you'll be led by what you find. There isn't an expectation of perfection; instead, you are just tearing, cutting, pasting, and watching something come to life. I personally just start pasting things into the front inside cover of my journal. Then, I might add some words and doodles, stickers, or stamps. It's a colorful way for me to take ownership from the very beginning of my journal.

FIGURE 1.4 Here is an inside cover collage from one of my journals. What do you notice? Do you see any patterns? What does it tell you about me?

HOW CREATIVITY AND REFLECTION LEAD TO PRODUCTIVITY

When you are done, take a step back and see if any patterns emerge. If you can't see it and you feel comfortable doing so, show it to a colleague or friend and see if they notice any patterns. Often, the things we tear and cut out of magazines mean something to us. If a lot of what you paste is nature, maybe ask yourself how you are making being out in nature a priority for you. If it's fashion, or people, or words about family or love, same question: How are you making it a priority?

**Creativity Collage Challenge, Tutorial Video**

Watch a video on how I do my inside journal covers. Let's get creative together!

Can you see any patterns that have to do with the school year? Do you see any images that could represent things you value in the classroom for yourself and your planning, for your students, or for upcoming projects? I have recently been reading a lot on equitable grading, and a part of that work is looking for your values in the classroom. What standards and pieces of the curriculum are of value to you and your population of students? Can you see any connections in your collage to that concept?

## STUDENT CREATIVITY COLLAGE

**FOR STUDENTS**

The same challenge you have just done in your journal is a great activity for students to do on the covers or inside covers of the notebooks they use in your class. This helps students have more ownership over their journals and feel invested in their continued use. They have personalized their journal by decorating it, an activity that may encourage more creativity in the pages inside. The more creative challenges you pose for your students the more they will be creative and take risks. Just like us! I would suggest giving your students reflective writing prompts as well. Why did students choose the images they did for their journal in your class? This extra step could even help you get to know your students a bit more.

# UNPLUG CHALLENGE

In this challenge, we are going to spend a full week tracking the following things:

- Getting eight hours of sleep

- Finding pockets of creativity in the mundane

- Putting the phone down during high-volume time after 7 p.m.

- Spending an hour being creative instead of scrolling

The idea is to get a feel for a few different activities that you wouldn't mind doing for a longer period of time. In order to form a habit, you need to do something over and over again for an average of about two months; we are just dipping our toes into these ideas to see if they work for us.

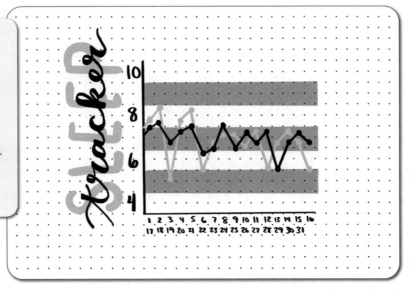

**FIGURE 1.5**
I often track how many hours I sleep at night. Here is an example showing sleep over a month with my goal being eight hours. I used an alarm app, my current favorite is called Sleep Cycle, to track my time asleep. Can you think of a way you might track your sleep?

Some specific ideas:

- Create a way to track your sleep. See figure 1.5 for some ideas.
- Try not to check your email right when you wake up. Instead, get up, drink a glass of water, and write a short journal entry on what you hope to accomplish that day.
- Pick a time of day (perhaps in the early morning or after dinner) to take a walk outside and away from your screen!
- Take a moment each day to doodle, paint, collage, use your pens, write out a quote, or add something else creative to your journal.

## WALK TO CREATE

A Stanford study found that walking can increase creativity by sixty percent, so take a moment before you get creative and go for a quick wander. Walking on a treadmill as well as walking outside can produce the same result. The idea is that when you walk, you are engaging several parts of your brain, so when you come back to be creative and start to do some divergent thinking, you are tapping into multiple parts of your brain that might not have been activated before your walk!

Meditative walking can give you a kind of "cognitive pause," helping to relieve tension in the muscles. It can have a rhythm or cadence. Create or find a meditative playlist—I have shared one below—turn on the music, walk for a bit, and then come back to your journal. Some suggestions:

- Add a collage and/or doodles.
- Brainstorm, make a list of whatever you are thinking about without limiting or editing yourself.
- Make a new to-do list.
- Write a reflection on your day.
- Write down any thoughts you had while on your walk, or things you noticed while you were walking.

Walking Meditation Playlist

This playlist accessible on Spotify has over twenty hours of music for non-static mediation. The Calm app has music options for mediation that you may also want to try.

# SOCIAL MEDIA INSPIRATION CHALLENGE

Let's take a closer look at some inspiration on social media in order to get our creative juices flowing. I love getting on social media—whether that is Pinterest, Instagram, or Twitter—or even doing a search on Google to generate ideas and see what others are doing. Through the internet I've connected with a community of other journalers and teachers who draw creativity and inspiration from one another. I enjoy commenting on people's posts and saving ideas for later use. There is rarely a time when I sit down to start creating a new layout or a monthly setup that I don't first go to social media for inspiration. Let's start building your own online community.

Here is your challenge:

- Follow at least five people participating in a social media community you'd like to be involved in. Some of my favorites are:
  **@alexandra_plans**
  **@amandarachlee**
  **@bulletsandconfetti**
  **@jashiicorrin**
  **@barbarahaegerart**
- Like four posts from their discussions.
- Follow two or three relevant hashtags. Some that I follow are: **#bujo**, **#teacherbujo**, **#bulletjournal**, and **#bulletjournalspreads**
- Comment on a few posts to start engaging in the community.

### Social Media Resources

Want access to more of my favorite sources of inspiration on social media? Scan the QR code for more information!

# Layouts to Get Started

Another thing that I usually include at the beginning of my journals is a year at glance page, which is just a single page that includes all the months in a mini format so that I can use it for reference when creating other spreads. It can help with planning to quickly find the start and end dates of each month and where they fall in the week, for instance, September starts on a Thursday this year.

### Year at a Glance Printable

Go to this post to see a monthly printable to make your year at a glance or future log a breeze to create. I also include links to sticker paper or double-sided sticky tape that makes creation in your journal limitless!

### FIGURE 1.6

In this simple one-page layout I write out the months of the year so that I can easily see way days of the week the months start as I fill in other pages throughout my use of the journal. These can be time-consuming, so I have found ways to make it go faster, like using stamps and stickers.

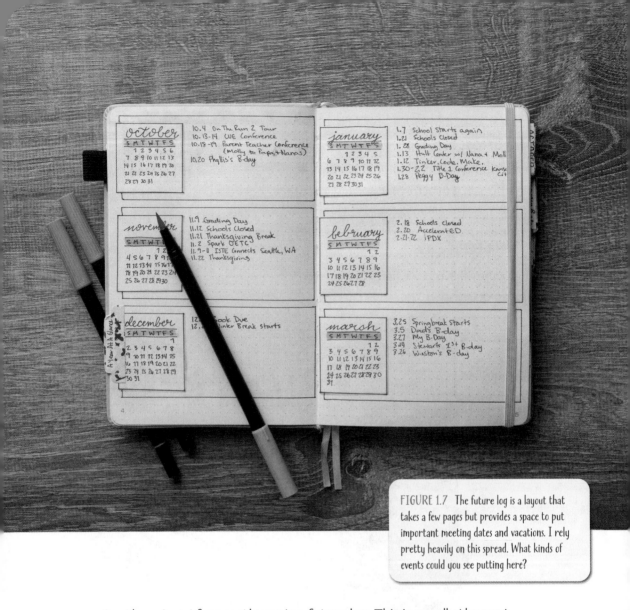

FIGURE 1.7 The future log is a layout that takes a few pages but provides a space to put important meeting dates and vacations. I rely pretty heavily on this spread. What kinds of events could you see putting here?

Another piece I frequently use is a future log. This is usually the next few pages in my journal. This is where I write important dates, like school closures, birthdays, vacation dates, etc. To get some inspiration on this go onto your favorite social media site or app and type in the words "Year at a Glance Bullet Journal®" or "Future Log Bullet Journal®" and see what pops up. I would love to see what you have come up with so use the hashtag #teacherjournaling and tag me so I can see!

# Making Time for Self-Reflection

One of the most important parts of the Four Stage Learning Cycle by David Kolb is the act of reflection. Learning doesn't happen by just doing it; you have to think about the experience, what you learned, and what your plans are for the next step. We know that reflection is key to learning, but for some reason it is always the first thing to go when we are stretched for time, both for ourselves and for our students.

When we are truly reflecting, it's like we are looking into a mirror thinking about our learning experience, such as how it looked, how it felt, and how it might inspire us in the future. Sometimes we ask others for feedback, sometimes we let loose and write our feelings, sometimes we use prompts to get us going, and sometimes we reflect on data.

Often, the process of reflecting relies on you to describe the situation or learning, what you were feeling, what was good and bad about the learning, or problems you might have had. Then you move on to the planning stage: what conclusions can you draw, what can you do to fix the problems—what are your solutions?

**Reflective practice** is "learning through and from experience towards gaining new insights of self and practice" (Finlay, 2008). For educators, this process can help you understand yourself and the way you teach, and it helps you hone your craft. By asking yourself questions, you can start to figure out your strengths and what might need work. What do you want to track and focus on? Then out of that comes innovation, it can help you try new things, adapt and change what isn't working, and focus on your goals.

**Reflection Writing Layouts Inspiration**

Want more ideas on how to include reflection writing into your journal? Scan the QR code to see example layouts that feature reflective writing.

Many of us know that writing can be therapeutic, and we as educators can use it to our advantage. When you get down to it, you know that when prompting yourself to think about what is going on in your life, such as issues you might be having and things that you really want, we often want to see it in black and white on paper. You either want to dump out your feelings or create a list of pros and cons. Something about putting our thoughts and reflections down on paper makes us think more critically and intentionally about what is on our minds, and more importantly, how to address it. There was a study done in the '90s at the University of Amsterdam where the participants were asked to write in order to study how it affected their thoughts. They found that after only a few writing sessions, the participants were "less anxious, tense, tired, and depressed" (Smit & Van der Hulst, p. 105). After the last few years teaching during the COVID-19 pandemic, I believe teachers are feeling more stress and strain than ever before. Rather than carrying that stress around with us, it might be helpful to try getting it out on the page.

When you're ready to dive deeper into this, scan the QR code to see examples of layouts to try in your own journal.

Perhaps, after trying a few small writing reflections in your journal, you are thinking you would like to go a step further. I once signed up for a free twenty-day journaling prompt email, and I loved it. I got to not only reflect but also add fun little creative additions to those entries. These particular prompts were just about life in general and not about teaching or education, but I have now gone ahead and created my own educator's version. The following prompts are based on the mindful analysis approach.

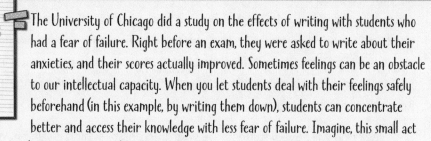

The University of Chicago did a study on the effects of writing with students who had a fear of failure. Right before an exam, they were asked to write about their anxieties, and their scores actually improved. Sometimes feelings can be an obstacle to our intellectual capacity. When you let students deal with their feelings safely beforehand (in this example, by writing them down), students can concentrate better and access their knowledge with less fear of failure. Imagine, this small act of taking time out before an exam and letting students free write about their anxiety or fear about their upcoming test can actually allow them to do better on said test. It's so simple! I encourage you to try this out with your students right before their next test.

## Mindful Analysis Approach

The **mindful analysis** approach is based in Buddhist philosophy, and includes four phases.

- Phase one is focusing on your current situation, really drilling down into what is happening in your life right now. Doing this in your own words is incredibly important.

- Phase two helps you focus on how you got to where you are now. It's important that your focus be related to what you talked about in phase one, gathering ideas of what is causing tensions or sending you in the wrong direction. It is helpful in this phase to examine things carefully and in-depth in a way that is comfortable to you.

- Phase three is all about processing your emotions and seeing connections to what the second phase brought up that might have been a bit of a surprise. Hopefully, you'll start developing some tasks and goals to help feel like you have things under control again and can focus more peacefully on new targets and goals.

- Phase four is your own call to action—that is, what you will decide to do and act on. Commit to some of the things you want to accomplish.

I have taken this concept and adapted the prompts and questions to focus on your life as an educator. I've created a 28-day daily reflection, where you'll receive an email each day with a prompt for reflection. If you are interested, use the QR code to sign up. I encourage you to find a time that works for you, set a timer for ten minutes, and just write. Carve out a section in your journal—add a fun title or some stickers and washi tape if you fancy it—and just let your thoughts flow.

- Week one will have you describe your current teaching position. What do you teach, what hats do you wear in your building, etc.?

- Week two will have you focus more inwardly. What are your own personal goals, and how does your past influence who you are as a teacher?

- Week three has you discovering your own options based your perceived ideals for education and your classroom.

- Week four is a call to action. How might you go about making those goals a reality for you?

- And finally, week five is a closing reflection on what you have learned about yourself through the process. If at any time you don't like a prompt, you can just freewrite instead, as we might often have our students do. You have already set aside the time for yourself; use it to your advantage.

**28-Day Email Prompt**

Struggling with making time for reflection? I can help! Sign up for a daily writing prompt.

#  Chapter 1 Key Points

Here are the important takeaways from this chapter:

- Dot journaling is any kind of journaling that allows you to create priority-based lists in a plain journal (that you can add doodles, drawings, stickers and washi tape to and personalize to your heart's content; or keep it minimalistic). It's all about creating a journal that will work for you and your needs rather than buying a premade journal.

- Creativity can lead to satisfaction and productivity; you can set time aside for yourself to help reflect and prioritize your to-do list as well as your goals.

- Self-reflection can help you identify your own personal and professional goals and limits; it is an important part of the learning cycle and shouldn't be overlooked.

#  ISTE Standards Addressed

This chapter addresses several ISTE Standards, including:

### 2.1 Learner

Educators continually improve their practice by learning from and with others and exploring proven and promising practices that leverage technology to improve student learning. Educators:

a. Set professional learning goals to explore and apply pedagogical approaches made possible by technology and reflect on their effectiveness.

### 2.3 Citizen

Educators inspire students to positively contribute to and responsibly participate in the digital world. Educators:

d. Create experiences for learners to make positive, socially responsible contributions and exhibit empathetic behavior online that build relationships and community.

### 3.3 Empowering Leader

Leaders create a culture where teachers and learners are empowered to use technology in innovative ways to enrich teaching and learning.

a. Empower educators to exercise professional agency, build teacher leadership skills and pursue personalized professional learning.

 Reflection

Take some time to consider how the ideas in this chapter apply within your context using the questions below.

- What is your "why" for starting to tap into your creative and reflective self?
- What are some things you would like to focus on moving forward, both professionally and personally?
- Explore some of the links shared. Was there a creativity challenge, playlist, or activity that resonated with you? Why?

Share your reflections and thoughts online using the hashtag **#teacherjournaling**.

"What people have the capacity to choose, they have the ability to change." - Madeleine K. Albright

## NOTES & DOODLES

- make a habit

- mental inventory

| Need to do | Should be doing | Want to do |
|---|---|---|

Is it vital?
Does it matter? → no to both it's a distraction.
Cross off your list

Goals - break down into small projects
- no barriers  - clear defined tasks
- should take less than a month to complete

Reflect - Declutter your mind by creating a mental inventory. Get rid of things that don't matter.

Ideate - Focus on things that interest you by designing small, actionable projects

Dedicate - Get into a daily habit of updating your mental inventory.

# Time Management
## STRATEGIES

THE B

|  | |
|---|---|
| **do** IT NOW | **plan** IT |
| **delegate** IT | **delete** IT |

1 | 2
3 | 4

↑ IMPORTANT

← URGENT ─

NOT IMPORTANT | IMPORTANT

1 When is my deadlines? Are others waiting?
2 Will this help achieve goals 6 months from now?
3 Am I the only one who can complete this?
4 What happens if I don't get this done?

# CHAPTER 2
# Goal Setting

## CHAPTER OBJECTIVES

- Understand why setting goals is important for both teachers and students, and how to get started with a few simple strategies
- Know more about metadata and effect size, as well as how they relate to strategies used in the classroom
- Learn about Kanban boards for goal setting and project management and how you might create those in your journal, or by using digital platforms individually or with your team or department
- Consider the usefulness of habit tracking and how it relates to meeting your goals and forming the habits you want to see in your life

## SUPPLY LIST

- blank journal
- pens
- highlighters
- ruler
- smartphone

## VOCABULARY

- collection spread
- effect size
- growth mindset
- Kanban board
- teacher clarity

**G**oal setting can help us visualize the progress we want to see in our professional and personal lives. The act of setting goals can also provide clarity around what we do, our roles. It can also help us recognize and understand our own growth, offering an opportunity for reflection that can be just as important as the completion of a goal.

# Why Goal Setting Is Important for Teachers

As teachers, we can often feel micromanaged or like we don't always have agency in our jobs. Sometimes it feels as if there's no forward movement or ability to improve or change our practice. We may be asked to provide yearly goals to our administration but more often than not, those goals are written down in September and not thought about again until later in the year for formal observation. However, what we have learned from visible learning researcher John Hattie is that when you set goals for learning and your own professional growth, that goal setting can have a measurable impact.

## Measuring Impact through Effect Size

For those of you that haven't heard of **effect size** before, it's basically a measure of how significant an approach is compared to standard practice. Hattie synthesized the results (meta-analysis) of numerous research studies on different influences on student learning (class size, feedback, challenge of goals, etc.) and measured their effect sizes, publishing the results and ranking the various approaches from most effective to least effective.

Put in another context, effect size can be used to measure the severity of earthquakes, tornadoes, and hurricanes. What we know about a category 4

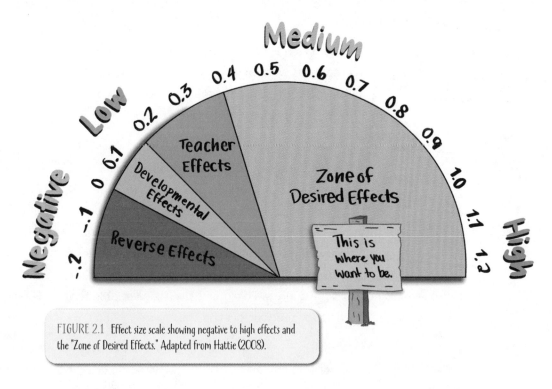

FIGURE 2.1  Effect size scale showing negative to high effects and the "Zone of Desired Effects." Adapted from Hattie (2008).

hurricane tells us how to prepare for the oncoming storm. Similarly, when we understand the effect size of a classroom strategy, we can determine if it's worth the effort to focus on it or not.

When we talk about effect size on teaching, we want to be in what Hattie calls the "zone of desired effects" (see figure 2.1). Anything with a 0.4 rating or higher is in this zone and does a world of good in the classroom, while anything below that doesn't produce the desired results. Hattie calls the average effect size of 0.4 the "hinge point."

To break down the effect size scale a little more, notice the reverse effects section in red. Those could be things like lack of sleep (-0.05) or punishment at home for poor behavior at school (-0.33). These obviously have negative effects on student outcomes. Teacher effects are things that we often think have huge impacts in the classroom that actually don't, such as individualized instruction (0.22) or use of a PowerPoint in class (0.26). What we find difficult to find time for during class—or in some cases, aren't given the professional

freedom to do—can often have a huge impact, such as teachers working together to evaluate their lessons (0.93), students seeking help from peers (0.83), or classroom discussion (0.82).

By measuring your learning and growth goals in this way, you can better commit to achieving goals—and even setting goals that are more likely to be reached. You should always be cautious of over interpreting the data, however. For example, providing feedback to students has an effect size of 0.73, but if you give that feedback months later, it isn't nearly as helpful to students. Therefore, time is a variable that can drastically change the effect of feedback in the classroom.

Hattie's research specifically calls out the importance of **teacher clarity**, or the concept that the teacher knows their content and what they are doing in the classroom, and understands the success criteria for students to achieve learning goals. In essence, teacher clarity is saying: "This is what we are doing; I am being clear and about our goals and standards; and this is what we all have to do as a community to get there." Teacher clarity can impact a classroom with a 0.75 effect size, even larger than goal setting alone. However, you can't have teacher clarity without first having goals, which are important for you as a professional but also for students.

## Goal Setting for Reflection and Growth

I have gotten better over the years about setting goals for myself and achieving them. All of my achievements have come from brainstorming and thinking about where I want to go, knowing what I need and how to get there, having a way to track my progress, and then figuring out how to continue. I have become very good at self-starting a new goal or project. This has become second nature to me now, but it is something I have been working on for over a decade. I have had many conversations and brainstorming sessions with peers to work out these building blocks, asking: "What should we do next?" "Where are we going?" and "How do we get there?" At a district level I would hope teacher leaders, instructional coaches, and administrators are asking these types of questions all the time.

In the book *Developing Assessment Capable Visible Learners*, Douglas Fisher, Nancy Frey, and John Hattie talk about the following things being needed for learning and growth. These five things have everything to do with goal setting and reflection:

1. I know where I'm going.
2. I have the tools for the journey.
3. I monitor my progress.
4. I recognize when I am ready for what is next.
5. I know what to do next (2018).

At the classroom level, teachers are great at this when thinking about standards-based teaching and backward lesson design. We do these things all the time when lesson planning; we just need to learn how to apply them in other areas of our lives.

When we set goals with intention instead of just as a reaction, we are much more likely to achieve them. With intentionality in brainstorming, you can create goals that are all yours.

We are often asked to write goals for our yearly evaluations, and then we forget about them for the rest of the year. It is hard to track and visualize goals when they are made at one point in time and then never revisited. Journaling, and more specifically goal setting can help with this. By bringing those goals front and center, it becomes easier as the more goals you set and attain, the more you revisit and think about them. It also becomes easier to see your potential flourish for what you are actually doing and accomplishing on a daily basis.

**FOR STUDENTS**

Students tend to meet the expectations that they and others have set for them, so goal setting is extremely important. By third grade, students have a pretty accurate sense of how to set their own goals and achieve them. According to Fisher, Frey, and Hattie, "Students set themselves expectations about what and how they can achieve and by age eight, these are pretty accurate" (2018).

Additionally, setting goals that are achievable but just enough of a challenge is incredibly important. We want to set realistic expectations, but also avoid students being bored in the classroom. Boredom actually has a reverse effect size in the classroom. Finding that "Goldilocks zone" goal is essential, and it takes practice. As a teacher, you should start by routinely setting goals for yourself to get the feel of it before you begin guiding students through the process. Students want (and need) school to be challenging, but not so challenging that they feel defeated. Goals that are challenging but attainable are essential to a growth mindset.

Some tips for promoting student goals:

- Focus on the learning, not just the "correct" end product.
- Use the SMART goal setting system (SMART stands for Specific, Measurable, Attainable, Relevant, and Time-based). Using this system helps create goals that can be met and creates a habit around goal setting. Teach them the system, but let them create the goals. Scan the QR code for a video on SMART goal setting.
- Capture the learning opportunities.
  - Devote some time in class to come back to these goals and have students think about where they are in terms of meeting them, focusing on the learning that is taking place at this point, not just that they have completed or finished the goal. This is one of the most important aspects of goal setting. Coming back to the goal and evaluating.
  - Identifying successes and roadblocks helps with the measurement of the goal being attained.
  - This takes some practice. We aren't used to calling out these learning moments. The more we highlight it as teachers, the more students will pick up on it.

- Cultivate time in your lesson plans not just on goal setting but also on self-reflection. Self-reflection allows for students to be more aware of their learning, as well as how to stay active in their learning goals and how to change things up when they hit roadblocks.

One additional caveat to goal setting with students is the need for "just-in-time" feedback. Feedback doesn't have to come just from teachers; it can also come from self-reflection and from peers. Often we focus on feedback from just one source: teacher to student. We need to challenge ourselves to give more time in class for self-reflection and peer feedback. Students need to learn the skills of providing peer feedback; we learn more from our peers and from our own self-reflection than we can from just teacher feedback. When students know they are creating a product that will be looked at by an authentic audience or their peers, they will often give a better final product and take the feedback more seriously than when it is just turned in to the teacher.

How To Set SMART Goals

Watch the video for additional advice on setting SMART goals.

Showing students how to document their progress and track their successes is important. You have to find a time to revisit these goals, however. Don't just give it a single ten-minute activity and forget about it; come back to it at the end of the week or grading period and have students reflect on how they did on that particular goal. This kind of journaling is really suited for the beginning of the week or beginning of the period. In secondary school, it is a great activity to do in advisory or homeroom periods, and you can also use time to have students reflect and pair up to problem-solve how to get through roadblocks on their goals. This is a great way to foster a communal mindset and have students thinking about improvement—when we know how to articulate our goals and how to achieve those goals, we all do better as a community.

From research on visible learning we know that goal setting can have an effect size of 0.56. We know setting SMART goals are helpful; we just have to prioritize time to do those tracking and goal-setting activities with students.

# Setting up Your Journal to Facilitate Goal Setting

A helpful first step in setting up your journal for goal setting is to create a "brain dump" page just for goals. I love putting these at the front of my journal to go back and add to, or reference at any time. The first fifty pages of my journal are often devoted to things that help me throughout the year and are not tied to a specific date or time. These are often referred to as **collection spreads**, or pages that go into every journal you start. I usually add a brain dump page for each of my big projects as a catchall for ideas and brainstorms (see figure 2.2).

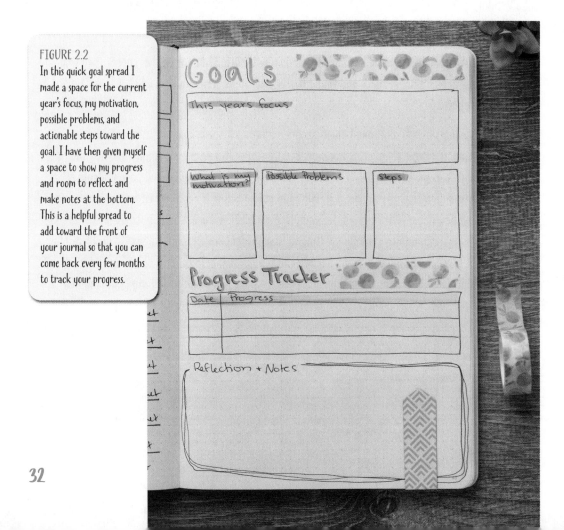

**FIGURE 2.2**
In this quick goal spread I made a space for the current year's focus, my motivation, possible problems, and actionable steps toward the goal. I have then given myself a space to show my progress and room to reflect and make notes at the bottom. This is a helpful spread to add toward the front of your journal so that you can come back every few months to track your progress.

# BEGIN WITH A BRAINSTORM

Create a page dedicated to brainstorming your goals for the coming year.

Ask yourself what you can focus on this year. Keep in mind your own personal goals, what you are able to control, and what is achievable for you.

After you have a few goals identified, ask: "Why do I want to spend time on this goal?"

---

### TROUBLE BRAINSTORMING?

As mentioned in the previous chapter, meditation can help unlock your creativity and brainstorming capabilities. Try to do a small breathing meditation before doing your goal-setting brainstorm.

One of my favorite ways to meditate is to do guided meditation with the Calm app. I love their daily meditations and the Daily Trip meditation series. They also have a meditation on harnessing creativity, which is only fourteen minutes.

Calm App on
the App Store

---

## HOW TO DO QUICK GOAL SETTING IN ANY JOURNAL ACROSS SUBJECT AREAS

Many students at the middle and high school level have a spiral notebook to use as a journal for each class. Some elementary and middle schools will also buy premade journals or planners. For a regular spiral, you can dedicate a page to the following activity. For those that are using a premade planner, you will have to look for a column on the left or right side of the page that will work. Notebooks often have spaces for weekly spelling words or notes, or columns for Saturdays and Sundays that rarely get used. Here are some areas where students can do some goal setting and habit tracking to help with time management:

- Academic goals for the week (how much studying, reading, homework, etc.)
- Social life (how much time you have for socializing, which friends you need to connect with, etc.)
- Exercise or sports (how much daily exercise you need, how much time for sports practice, etc.)
- Long-term academic plans (what grades you would like to see in classes and how can you make that happen)

These could be writing prompts for their journal, or you could show them how to make a quick water tracker in their journal (figure 2.3) and have them track their water intake.

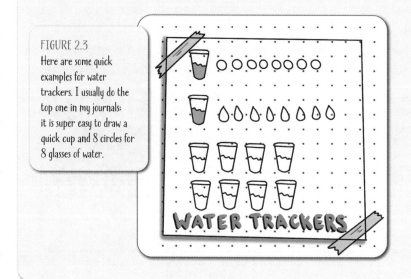

FIGURE 2.3
Here are some quick examples for water trackers. I usually do the top one in my journals; it is super easy to draw a quick cup and 8 circles for 8 glasses of water.

# Identify Your Goals

Teachers are usually asked to come up with at least two or three goals for the year based on some metric that they have been assigned. My district uses the Five Dimensions of Teaching and Learning (5D) rubric, but I know many other districts use the Marzano Teacher Evaluation Model. The Marzano method is meant to simplify the teacher evaluation process for both teachers and administrators. You're observed based on specific standards that are supposed to provide a feedback framework to teachers. The 5D rubric is similar, using a set of standards for teachers that came out of the University of Washington. I suggest looking up your observation protocols or rubric before starting.

FIGURE 2.4  In my school district we use the 5D rubric as our teacher evaluation and goal setting system. I took some time to write out the standards and add in an image of puzzle pieces. This would be a page to go back to when I am working on my beginning of the year teacher goals.

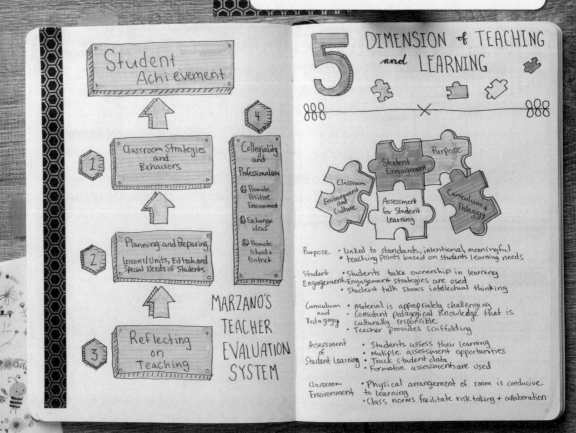

Student Achievement

1 Classroom Strategies and Behaviors

2 Planning and Preparing
Lessons/Units, Ed Tech and Special Needs of Students

3 Reflecting on Teaching

4 Collegiality and Professionalism
- Promote Positive Environment
- Exchange ideas
- Promote School + District

MARZANO'S TEACHER EVALUATION SYSTEM

5 DIMENSION of TEACHING and LEARNING

Classroom Environment and Culture · Student Engagement · Purpose · Assessment for Student Learning · Curriculum + Pedagogy

Purpose
- Linked to standards, intentional, meaningful
- Teaching points based on students learning needs

Student Engagement
- Students take ownership in learning
- Engagement strategies are used
- Student talk shows intellectual thinking

Curriculum and Pedagogy
- Material is appropriately challenging
- Consistent pedagogical knowledge that is culturally responsible
- Teacher provides scaffolding

Assessment of Student Learning
- Students assess their learning
- Multiple assessment opportunities
- Track student data
- Formative assessments are used

Classroom Environment
- Physical arrangement of room is conducive to learning
- Class norms facilitate risk taking + collaboration

## 3-2-1 ACTIVITY

Ryder Carroll in his book *The Bullet Journal Method* talks about a 5-4-3-2-1 activity. When I came upon this strategy I was gobsmacked! I have been using a method like this for a while. As a district-level employee, I have constantly been asking myself and my colleagues, "Where do we want teachers to be in three years?" This helps me plan the PD and the support needed to get us there. Without a vision as a district, you can struggle with everything: communication, reliable support, and follow-through. I have modified Carroll's idea based on what I have already been doing for the last couple of years. If having a random brainstorm page does not work for you, then this might be the ticket to get you going. This will work best across a two-page spread. First, split your page into three rows as shown in figure 2.5. Write "3 Years" on the first row, "2 Months" on the second row, and "1 Day" on the third, then answer the questions:

- 3 Years: Where do you see yourself (or your department/team) in three years?

- 2 Months: What do you want to accomplish in the next two months?

- 1 Day: What do you need to do in the next day?

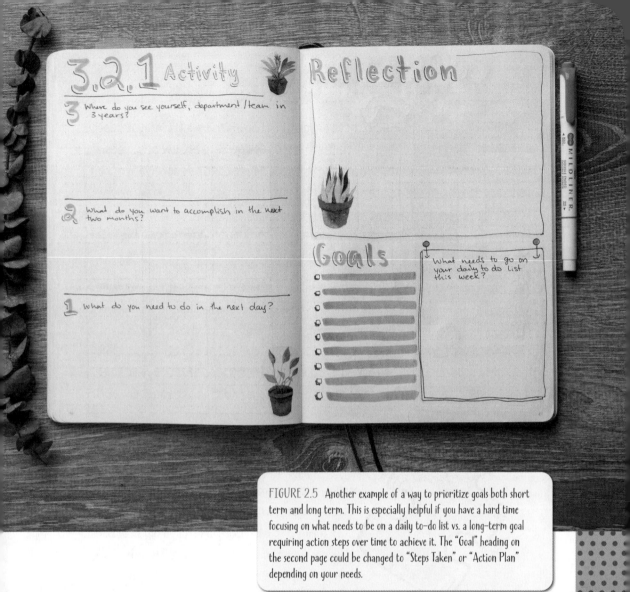

**3.2.1** Activity

**3** Where do you see yourself, department/team in 3 years?

**2** What do you want to accomplish in the next two months?

**1** What do you need to do in the next day?

Reflection

Goals

What needs to go on your daily to do list this week?

FIGURE 2.5 Another example of a way to prioritize goals both short term and long term. This is especially helpful if you have a hard time focusing on what needs to be on a daily to-do list vs. a long-term goal requiring action steps over time to achieve it. The "Goal" heading on the second page could be changed to "Steps Taken" or "Action Plan" depending on your needs.

If there's time, go back and prioritize your goals. Is there at least one in each section of your journal? On the second page, you can either use it as-is to freewrite your reflection or, if it helps, split it into three corresponding rows and reflect on your prioritized goals. If this reflection isn't sparking your imagination, consider going back to the brainstorming on the previous page. Were those goals as important as you thought? Or were they not articulated clearly enough or given enough direction?

# Break Goals into Chunks

A friend of mine once called me a juggling octopus. In this friendly analogy, she was trying to make a point about my multitasking; at any one time, I am working on at least eight different projects. My father has always written out a to-do list of chores and projects that need to get done that day. Regardless of how long the list for the day is, I guarantee you at some point I will find him power washing something that hadn't made it onto his list. I get my juggling octopus tendencies from him.

As I have been doing more research into productivity and efficiency, as I have watched the journaling community evolve on social media, and as I have done more reflection on my own personality and habits and where they might be coming from, I am not convinced I'm being as effective as I could be. Only about two percent of people can effectively multitask, and the rest of us are simply juggling, according to Ryder Carroll. To avoid this, we need to work on our intentionality by setting short goals (dare I say SMART goals?).

In order to start managing the larger goals (those in the "3 Year" section) we have to break them into smaller, more manageable chunks. I'll share an example of this. I once made it a goal to speak at a big national conference. This started because I had a coworker with whom I was very competitive. He was asked to speak at a big conference on a project he did with his students. The competitor in me wondered how he had this opportunity and I didn't, but I realized that no one was going to come and seek me out—I had to make it happen for myself.

I knew in order to get there I had to dive deeper into what made me a good teacher.

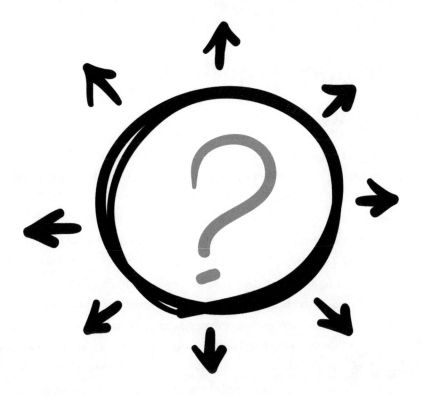

What was I passionate about? In what areas did I need to learn and grow in order to be a good speaker? I also knew that it would take practice, and I would have to start small. I began going to local professional development events, first as an attendee and then as a speaker. I set myself goals for regional conferences, and then eventually national and international conferences. I would tell myself that once I got accepted to speak at one conference, I would try for another, larger conference. I was building my confidence, learning how to be a better presenter, and giving myself time to refine topics that were relevant to classroom teachers. I was goal setting right and left!

In order to attain goals we need to be good at maximizing our time spent at work—getting really productive during our contract hours—so that we can be creative and happy in our lives outside of work. This is easier said than done, so we need to take a closer look at how to go about maximizing our productivity for how we function and the type of teacher schedules we have.

# Maximizing Productivity for Goal Setting

Research shows that we are at our most productive in the morning, which makes it a great time for reflective planning and setting the day's goals or tasks. Additionally, if there is a task that you have been avoiding that needs to get done, make sure to do it first, allowing other tasks that you're looking forward to in the afternoon to inspire you and keep you going. Unfortunately for many teachers, setting time aside in the morning might not be something that works with your schedule. Our prep periods often determine when we get a chance to work on things. Regardless of when you can find time in your schedule, the same metric applies: get the things done that you least want to do first, and then move on to the more fun things. Personal goals and tasks, as well as daily reflection and gratitude, are best done at the end of the day. We will go into time management in more detail in the next chapter.

It can be helpful to establish a goal-setting process in your journal so you understand how to approach different goals. Here are some suggestions for tackling yearly, monthly, and daily goals.

- **Yearly goals** can be made at any time. Most people set these kinds of goals in January for a fresh start or as a new year's resolution. For teachers, it generally makes sense to set yearly goals in September with the start of the new school year.

- **Monthly goals** are helpful to force yourself to think about your bigger yearly goals, and set actionable steps you would like to take toward them each month. When setting up a new month in my journal, I allow my yearly goals and my current projects to inform my monthly goals. Honestly, the season we are in can play a big role in this, too; my projects in the winter are entirely different than my projects in the summer.

- **Daily goals and to-do lists** help you maximize the actual time you have during the day. I love to think of my journal as a sieve or filter. I sometimes go back to my monthly goals, or to a page I always make at the front of my journal where I write down daily tasks. What can you get accomplished today? Is it Friday? Is that the day you make copies for the next week? Is it Wednesday? Do you need to do a load of laundry? While it might seem repetitive at times, it keeps those goals and projects front and center, and reminds me to get them done.

FIGURE 2.6 In this spread I worked on trying to develop a list of habitual tasks that I could stack on specific days to be able to handle my workload. What are things that you can do each day of the week to help spread your workload over the week?

**FOR STUDENTS**

If you have students for a homeroom or advisory period, I recommend doing a goal-setting lesson once every grading period. Give students space at the beginning of a new class schedule to write out what their day looks like, maybe even specifics about each teacher's turn-in and late policies, or the best way to contact them (by email or messaging through the school's online platforms).

Maybe add specific days for upcoming exams (this is more likely at the higher levels where an end-of-quarter/semester exam is standard) or even a section to list important dates, like grading days and no-school days for an at-a-glance reference.

**FIGURE 2.7**
In this example you can see how walking students through setting up a page like this in a spiral notebook is doable.

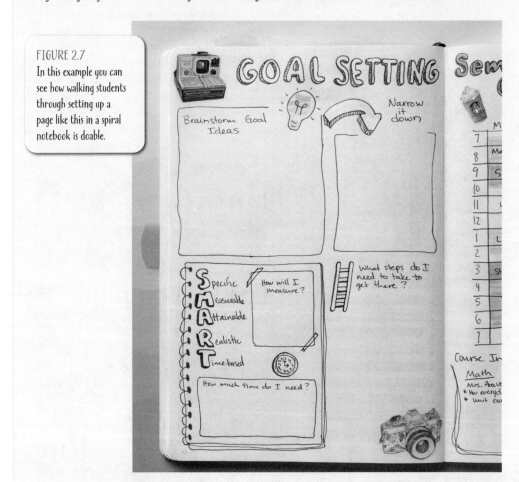

While having students draw this out you can set a timer for the brainstorming section and then explain how they might narrow their ideas. Do your own brainstorming and show how you might narrow that down into the smaller box. Then move to the SMART goals and while explaining the concept, have them decorate and fill in their pages.

This page will be good to come back to later on. You could have students do this at the beginning of a new unit or at the beginning of the school year for yearly goals. If students do this at the beginning of the unit, it may help to revisit the page halfway through the unit and again after they get feedback on their summative assignment. For yearly goals, I would revisit the goal page before the end of every grading period.

**Student Goal Setting Printable**

Follow this QR code to my website to download this printable.

FIGURE 2.8
Here is a similar layout that can be printed and used as a quick worksheet for students to fill out instead of doing it in their journal. Same end results, just different approaches.

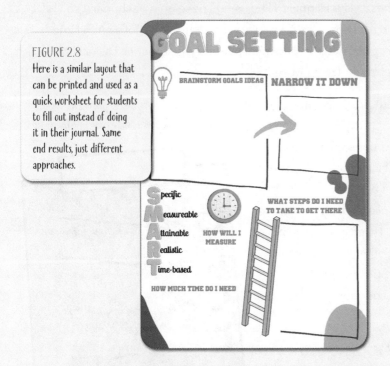

# Using a Kanban Board or "Teacher Dashboard" to Track Project Progress

A **Kanban board** is a project management tool that helps you better visualize what you are working on, limits the number of things you are currently working on, and maximizes your workflow. I tend to think of goals as projects, and I think understanding different ways to track or measure your movement on goal achievement is helpful. When I have used Kanban boards in my journal (I usually call them dashboards), there are certain components that are always present.

## Sticky Notes and Visual Markers

Project teams call these visual signals. I like using these on a dashboard so that I can use it again and again, putting down a fresh sticky note each time. These work well for repeated tasks like meal planning, or teacher tasks that have to be done repeatedly. (See figure 2.9.)

Sometimes people put limits on how many visual markers you can have on the board at any one time. Most of the time, I'm dealing with the constraints of my journal, which means I don't have room for too many sticky notes at a time. This is something to keep in mind: How many notes can you create before you are maxed out and can't be efficient anymore? This could also help you notice when you are getting close to burning out and committed to doing too much.

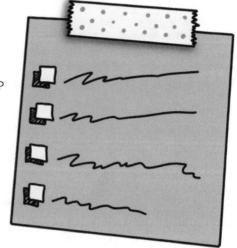

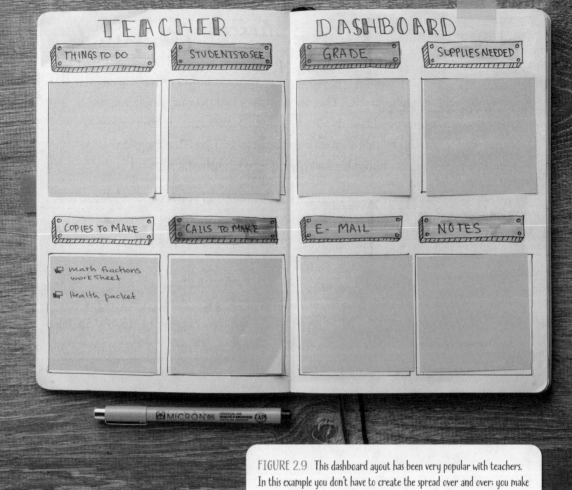

FIGURE 2.9 This dashboard layout has been very popular with teachers. In this example you don't have to create the spread over and over; you make it once and then just replace the sticky notes. Imagine being able to keep sticky notes off your desk and in an organized space in your journal! What categories would you use on your dashboard? What would you change?

## Columns or Quadrants

Another thing frequently seen in a Kanban board is the use of columns to represent a specific activity, or to show the workflow or passage of time. Instead of the activities in the teacher dashboard example, you could list the days of the week with a sticky note for each.

In figure 2.10 the quadrants are being used to help you differentiate what is or isn't urgent—with a "Do It Now" or "Delete It" category. Notice too that on the Time Management Strategies page there is a section designated for "Delete It" or "Delegate It." This comes back to knowing when you need to let go of a project or filter it out of your tasks because it isn't actually something you need to complete, or it's something you don't have the capacity to do and it should be delegated to a teammate instead.

The key aspect of the Kanban board is to know when you have completed a task. Sometimes I will put multiple tasks on a sticky note and cross or check them off once completed. Then, when the sticky note is done, I will pull it

FIGURE 2.10 This is a specific example to help with big projects. It could also be used with a department or team, or when looking at larger personal goals.

off the board and throw it away or replace it with a new one. If you feel like you would rather see that completion pile up, then you could add a "Done" column and put the stickies there. To start simple, you could create a column on your board for each stage of your projects:

- on deck

- up next

- in progress

- done

Link to Trello website

Trello is a website that allows you to use columns and cards to manage projects and tasks. It is a way to do a digital Kanban board.

There are, of course, digital options for Kanban boards if you would like to try this out online. I have personally tried Trello and Asana. While Trello is more visual with its cards and columns, Asana works better with a larger team. So if you are looking for something to use with a team of people I would start there. If you would prefer to use a product that is similar to sticky notes on a desk, start with Trello and see how you like it.

I like to do a review of my projects at the end of each month to see how they are progressing. This is usually a simple one-page layout with a few boxes for updates, for example:

- projects that were completed this month

- things that I would like to start next month

- things that are still in progress.

End-of-the-Month Project Review

Go to my website to see examples of layouts. I use for tracking progress on projects and reviewing them at the end of the month.

I also leave room to reflect on habits to start, stop, or continue the next month. Scan the QR code to see some examples of those end-of-the-month review layouts on my website.

# Strategies for Habit Tracking

Forming a habit takes time, and working on acknowledging the habits you would like to cultivate (and those you would like to break) is step one. James Clear, author of *Atomic Habits: An Easy & Proven Way to Build Good Habits & Break Bad Ones*, says it takes more than sixty days to form a habit (2018). Obviously, this can vary greatly depending on the habit, the person involved, and the circumstances. When you work on tracking that habit, you are giving yourself immediate feedback, a sense of a reward for your effort that can accumulate over time. It keeps the habit in the forefront of your mind so you can keep working on it, and it can show you that you are on the right path to achieving the goal of kicking the bad habit or creating a new and better habit, whatever the case may be.

Seeing the habit tracker in my daily journal does a number of things:

- It reminds me to act. It's a visual cue to do the thing!

- It is motivating to check it off (or color it in, cross it out, etc.). I am a person that loves to check off boxes— what will help motivate you?

- It helps to see success in that moment, that day, or that week, depending on how you are tracking it.

There are so many things that you could turn into a habit tracker. I tend to consistently pay attention to how much rest I am getting and how much water I am drinking, but there are so many other things that you could track, as shown in table 2.1. You can also track things *not* to do, such as those examples shown with an asterisk.

**TABLE 2.1**    Examples of Habits to Track

| PERSONAL | TEACHERLY | HEALTH |
|---|---|---|
| Gratitude (a line a day) | Send three positive notes home a week | Eight hours of rest a night |
| Read five pages a day | Make a positive phone call home | Meditate each day |
| Write one page a day | Reflect on your lessons for the week | Move your body five times a week |
| Make your bed each morning | Go home at the end of your contract hours; don't stay late | Stretch your body |
| Prioritize your "me time" | Make your copies for the next day on your prep | Wake up by or go to bed by a specific time |
| One friend date a month | Read a few pages in a professional book | Make sure you take your vitamins |
| Clean the kitchen before bed | Watch an online lecture or PD | Take a walk three times a week |
| Call a parent once a week | Participate in a Twitter chat | 10,000 steps a day |
| Review your finances | *No purchasing teacher materials | *Cut back on soda, sugar or caffeine |
| *No online purchases or spending | *No purchasing stationery supplies (you know teachers love some good stationery!) | *No alcohol, smoking |

List of Habit Tracking Apps

In this blog post I list some of my tried and true apps that I use regularly to track habits.

Habits get easier the more you do them. Try and track the habits in the moment—and also try not to give yourself a hard time when you forget to track. You can always come back to it. There are some apps that can be really helpful for tracking a variety of habits. For instance, the alarm app I use tracks my sleep, so as long as I set my alarm, I can track how long I slept each night. There are apps you can use to track your water consumption; I have even gone so far as to buy an electronic water bottle that syncs with an app to automatically track how much I drink. Despite all this, I have found that good, old-fashioned daily tracking in my journal is what works best for me. I usually find a space in my daily tasks section to draw eight circles or water drops and color them in as I drink my water. I have tried other trackers, like Momentum for exercise, Habitshare (which is cool because you can make goals and share them with friends to motivate each other if that works for you), and the Done app, to name a few.

# SLEEP AND WATER TRACKING

Most adults don't get enough sleep, especially when dealing with everyday stress that is piled on top of anxiety from political unrest or global pandemics. When you don't get enough sleep, you can feel physically unwell and your mental health may suffer—you can struggle to process things and can become forgetful. Not drinking enough water can have negative effects as well. So in addition to tracking your sleep and water, here are some ideas to write down in your journal to see if it helps you catch those Zs a little better.

## Sleep Habits to Try

- **Try out a sound machine.** I have had the Quick Sleep app on my phone for the longest time. It has a series of background noises and allows you to mix and match different sounds. It was through this app that I realized there are different frequencies beyond just white noise; I actually prefer the lower tone of brown noise.

- **Try keeping your room at a cooler temperature.** Watch what you eat and drink before bed. Sometimes a snack helps before going to sleep, but for some people it can cause indigestion. Pay attention or log what you eat before bed for a week and see if you can spot a pattern. Likewise, watch what you drink in the hours leading up to bedtime. Does alcohol or caffeine play a part in your sleep patterns?

- **Try avoiding screens before bed.** Instead, do non-digital activities like writing your daily gratitude and/or reflection, or try reading before bed and see if that helps you fall asleep faster.

- **Try waking up at a specific time each morning.** I am constantly hitting the snooze button or sleeping to the last minute before heading to my first meeting, but I also love to enjoy a cup of coffee in the morning. If I set a routine up where I can wake up and drink a cup of coffee in my living room before I start the day, my mood is instantly lifted. If I get a good night's sleep the night before, waking up earlier for that cup of coffee can be very motivating. What could be your morning motivator?

# Water Habits to Try

- Get a small cup and place it in the bathroom. Every time you come into the bathroom, try drinking that amount of water before you leave. I have tried this and have seen my overall water intake increase dramatically!

- Buy yourself a new water bottle to fit your water habits. Do you like to drink really cold water? Look into a double insulated bottle that can keep ice all day long. I really like ice water while I am teaching, and all other times I like less cold water. I also prefer to drink water with a straw, so using a straw tends to get me to drink more.

- Think about a tracking system beyond your journal. You could go as simple as rubber bands around your water bottle. Put two or three rubber bands at the bottom of your bottle and every time you empty it, one of the rubber bands moves from the bottom to the top to count how many bottles you drink. There is also a popular half gallon or full gallon bottle that has time stamps on the side for motivation, or water tracker beads that can be added to the top of a bottle. I have even bought both an electronic water bottle and the Ulla smart hydration reminder—it has a little motion-sensitive timer on it that flashes to remind you it's been awhile since you had some water.

- If plain water is off-putting, look into a soda stream to make seltzer water, or try infusing your water. I love doing this in the summertime especially—my favorite combos are citrus paired with an herb but I love looking for inspiration online, and trying new combinations is motivating.

- Some apps to try include Daily Water Tracker Reminder, Hydro Coach, and Water Minder. I also set alarms on my phone for 10:30, 12:30, and 2:30 as water checks, which works really well as a reminder.

# Chapter 2 Key Points

- Goal setting can help us in understanding our role as a teacher, or as a student for the upcoming year or unit. It can help us with clarity. It can also help us with understanding our own growth, and how reflection can be just as important as the completion of a goal.

- Using systems like Kanban boards while working on a larger project or with a team can help you understand when to let go and when to delegate. These are things that can be accomplished in a journal or using digital platforms.

- Habit tracking can be an incredibly useful thing to help us measure our attempts at attaining goals. When we think about SMART goals, a big component is that we write goals that are measurable. Tracking our habits towards goals can help us get there. Looking at those habits over time can also help give us feedback on our daily patterns and how we might change or adjust them to get to our goals.

# ISTE Standards Addressed

This chapter addresses several ISTE Standards, including:

**2.1 Learner**

Educators continually improve their practice by learning from and with others and exploring proven and promising practices that leverage technology to improve student learning. Educators:

a. Set professional learning goals to explore and apply pedagogical approaches made possible by technology and reflect on their effectiveness.

### 2.3 Empowering Leader

Leaders create a culture where teachers and learners are empowered to use technology in innovative ways to enrich teaching and learning.

c. Inspire a culture of innovation and collaboration that allows the time and space to explore and experiment with digital tools.

 Reflection

After reading chapter 2, take some time to consider how you will apply some of the strategies to your own life and journal setup.

1.  How intentional have you been previously with goal setting in your life? Have you seen yourself making personal goals? What about professional goals?

2.  How often do you reflect on your goals and think about their effectiveness, or when you have achieved a goal and need to start a new one?

3.  How often do you have students set goals?

    a.  If this is not something you already do, do you think you can find a time to do this in the future with them?

    b.  If you already do this, do you have students create goals and consistently come back to them to see if they are achieving those goals?

4.  Have you thought about tracking goals, projects, and/or habits before? How do you see this working out for you? What pitfalls might you encounter? How can you set yourself up for success with your goals?

5.  Did you notice as you started tracking habits if there were any subtle changes to your mood, or how it made you feel physically (if you were tracking something like water intake or sleep)?

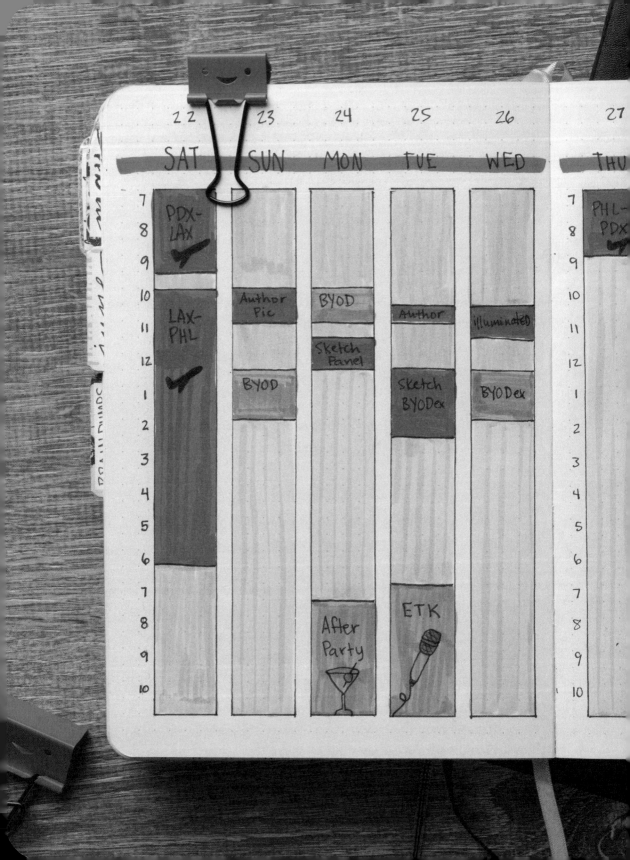

| 22 | 23 | 24 | 25 | 26 | 27 |
|----|----|----|----|----|----|
| SAT | SUN | MON | TUE | WED | THU |

**22 SAT**
- 7
- 8 — PDX-LAX ✈
- 9
- 10
- 11 — LAX-PHL ✈
- 12 ✔
- 1
- 2
- 3
- 4
- 5
- 6
- 7
- 8
- 9
- 10

**23 SUN**
- 10 — Author Pic
- 1 — BYOD

**24 MON**
- 10 — BYOD
- 11/12 — Sketch Panel
- 7/8 — After Party 🍸

**25 TUE**
- 10 — Author
- 1 — Sketch BYODex
- 7 — ETK 🎤

**26 WED**
- 10 — illuminated
- 1 — BYODex

**27 THU**
- 7
- 8 — PHL-PDX ✈
- 9
- 10
- 11
- 12
- 1
- 2
- 3
- 4
- 5
- 6
- 7
- 8
- 9
- 10

# CHAPTER 3
# Time Management

ST

nday
)am    ISTE author Pict
:30 pm

onday
)am
.30 am
.30 pm
:15 pm
45 pm
:00 pm
1:00 pm

esday
.30 am
.30 pm

45pm    FEN Happy hour
00pm    Ed tech Kareoke

dnesday
30 am
30 pm

## CHAPTER OBJECTIVES

- Learn how to utilize time blocking to get things done in a more efficient manner
- Discover some tips and tricks for using digital calendars, how to make them work better and harder for you
- Know how to be consistent in your planning, and what to look for to help with productivity
- Know what to look for in digital planners, including editable planners
- Learn how to do goal setting in any kind of journal for students
- Explore how to use technology to help with time management
- Discover how going paperless can actually provide students with quick, timely feedback, and also cut back on your grading time

## SUPPLY LIST

- blank journal with dot grid
- pens
- highlighters
- ruler
- phone or computer used for scheduling/reminders

## VOCABULARY

- calendex
- Pomodoro technique
- prospective memory
- time blocking
- ultradian rhythm

Ashley Whillans' book *Time Smart: How to Reclaim Your Time and Live a Happier Life* has an entire chapter on time affluence. According to Whillans, eighty percent of American workers feel "time poor," or that there is never enough time in the day to get all their responsibilities done. Research shows that it isn't often money that makes us happy; at least, not directly—it is when we have more leisure time to be present, rather than being trapped in the constant hustle. When you have time affluence, you are happier and can pursue activities you are passionate about. The way to become time affluent is similar to how you might take steps to better health: small habits and behavior changes. In talking about time affluence, we are talking about the things that you can control, what you are able to give priority to in your life. Your goal is to work toward having more, and better time for you, instead of constantly being stuck in time-consuming, unrewarding tasks.

# Time Blocking for Productivity

A couple of years ago, I was watching a YouTube video where a person was talking about **time blocking**. I thought, teachers blocking their time, of course! This is something students do that teachers should be utilizing more for our own tasks and projects. When you think about a student focusing on science for a one-hour block of time and then walking down the hall and working on math for the next block of time, focusing in the moment on that subject area, they are time blocking. Teachers naturally use time blocking techniques when focusing on planning for subjects in elementary, and periods in secondary, but we often don't think about it when it comes to our own individual tasks and planning our days. When you look at the time you have available to you in a day and wonder how you can possibly get it all done, one answer might be time blocking. In a nutshell, time blocking is setting manageable, bite-sized goals with time rather than tasks.

FIGURE 3.1  Not sure where to get started with time blocking? Begin by tracking your day-to-day activities to see where you spend the most time. In this example I wrote the days of the month down the page and the hours in each day horizontally. I chose a color blocking system for what I wanted to track and tried to diligently track what my days looked like. As you can see, I started strong at the beginning of the month and then didn't do very well at the end.

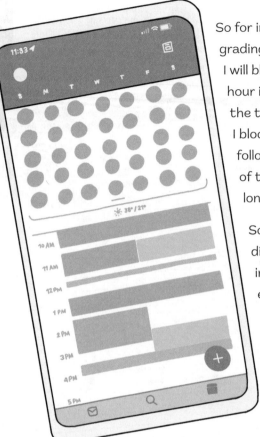

So for instance, if I know that I have to work on grading papers and I look at my available time, I will block out an hour for grading. When the hour is up, I will move on to my next task. If the task is not completed within the hour I blocked out, I need to look for time in the following day or week to add another block of time. I might also look into blocking out longer than an hour the next time.

Some tasks might require you to really dig in and take three hours or more. For instance, when I am lesson planning I easily need more than an hour. Knowing this and blocking enough time at the onset helps tremendously in achieving goals in a measurable time frame.

Other times, you might think a task is going to take a ton of time, but odds are it probably won't. For example, my child will often say she doesn't have time to unload the dishes; so I set a stopwatch. This was immensely helpful, showing her it only took her six minutes to unload the dishwasher, instead of dreading a task that she had built up in her head as taking a ton of time. Making it seem like a smaller, more manageable task helped get the job done. Ultimately this kind of learning helps students more instinctively know going forward how much time a task will take and it will be less daunting. They will be more apt to just jump right into the task in the future.

Time blocking only works if you build it up as a habit and make sure you focus on one thing at a time. As soon as you get distracted by something else, you lose your flow. The more present and focused you are on the task at hand, the more likely you are to unlock your creative and productive flow. Containing the activity or task in a set period of time allows you to bring your full attention to it.

# Time Blocking Using a Journal

When doing this in your journal—taking a look at your daily tasks, grouping items together, and then blocking out the time to get those things done— the most important part is estimating the amount of time needed to get those items done. When you know you have only thirty minutes to focus on a task, and you know what that task will be, you are more likely to use that time wisely. Even focusing for fifteen to thirty minutes on a task at a time can quickly add up, helping you get through your tasks with a feeling of accomplishment at the end of the day.

Don't forget to factor in non-work aspects of your life—family, social, and personal obligations and desires—that may take time away from scheduled tasks.

I would also recommend blocking out specific time for things that are tempting time wasters, like checking social media or shopping online. Noting these habits and setting aside time to do them makes them measurable and less likely to suck away at your time throughout the day. Instead, you can give that time back to yourself to do

### Forest App for Time Blocking

Something I love to use to help with my time blocking is the Forest app. I can specify the amount of time I need to focus on something, and the app locks my phone for the duration so I can't get distracted. If I stay on task and don't touch my phone, I grow a tree in the app. Eventually, if I use the app enough and continue to stay focused, I can plant a forest plants created by being on task. Additionally, Forest works with a real tree-planting organization called Trees for the Future, and plants trees while people use the app. It's a win-win for me!

something that brings you joy—which is the ultimate goal. If we have learned anything after the last few years of the pandemic, it is that we should value our time more; doing things we enjoy and spending our time with loved ones fills our cups more than the hustle.

# Time Blocking for Grading and Assessment

Time blocking also works for grading. Teachers are better able to handle large amounts of grading when we try batching it out. A small pile is easier to attack each day than a big stack of essays over the weekend. (As an English teacher, I did this for years and it was the worst part of my job.) When you divide up the work, each batch you complete gives you a sense of accomplishment and, over time, you can start to get that grading done

during contract hours and not have to take it home. Also, if you are attempting to give out assignments that only have to be marked right or wrong, have students help with that in class. If you are doing assignments that require more complex grading, try and work in time to conference with students and give small feedback throughout the project's duration, rather than one grade at the very end. This helps both of you: students learn better with formative feedback through the process.

Also remember that you don't have to grade everything, but if you're not grading traditionally, make sure you are clear with the students from the beginning what you will instead be looking for in a particular assignment. Teacher clarity has an effect size of 0.75, so don't underestimate how important that is in the classroom.

## START YOUR TIME BLOCKING JOURNEY

Create a page in your journal for today's daily tasks or your weekly tasks, depending on how much time you have available and how many items are on your to-do list.

- List out your tasks.

- Put a number next to them on the left-hand side to help you prioritize, if you didn't already write them down in order of urgency.

- On the right side of the list, put an estimate of how long you think each task will take you to get done. Use a different color if that helps it stand out.

- Look at your calendar and find chunks of time throughout the school day, your prep period, and after school to focus on getting these things done.

- Block it out on your digital calendar or write down when you plan to try and get it done this week.

- Try using the Forest app, a Pomodoro extension on your laptop, or something similar to help you focus and not get sucked into time-wasting sites or apps.
- If your timing was off (for instance, you thought going to the office to make some copies was going to take you twenty minutes and it only took ten), take note for next time.

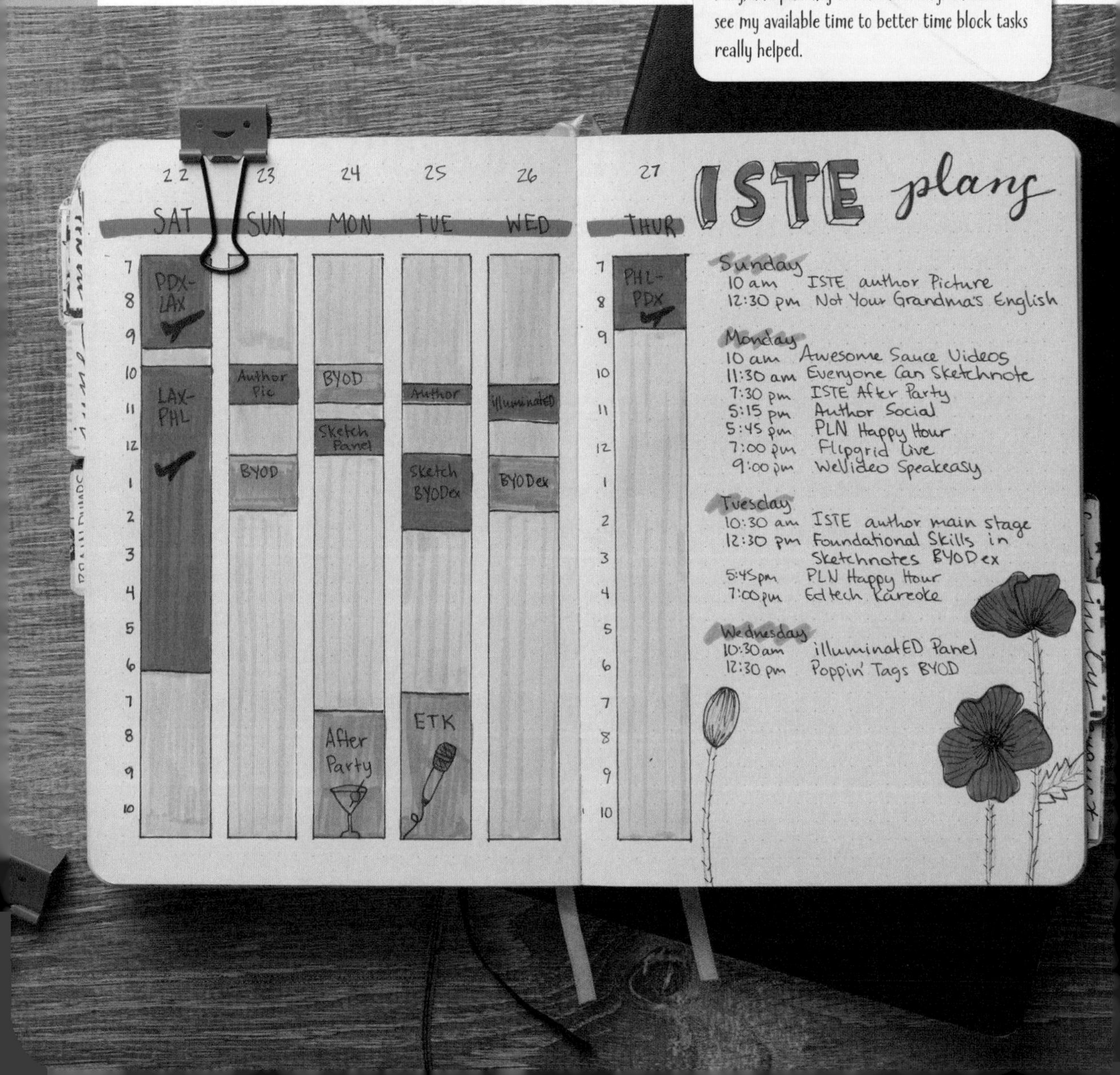

22 SAT
23 SUN
24 MON
25 TUE
26 WED
27 THUR
PDX-LAX
LAX-PHL
Author Pic
BYOD
BYOD
Sketch Panel
After Party
Author
Sketch BYODex
ETK
BYODex
PHL-PDX
ISTE plans
Sunday
10 am ISTE author Picture
12:30 pm Not Your Grandma's English
Monday
10 am Awesome Sauce Videos
11:30 am Everyone Can Sketchnote
7:30 pm ISTE After Party
5:15 pm Author Social
5:45 pm PLN Happy Hour
7:00 pm Flipgrid Live
9:00 pm WeVideo Speakeasy
Tuesday
10:30 am ISTE author main stage
12:30 pm Foundational Skills in Sketchnotes BYODex
5:45pm PLN Happy Hour
7:00pm Edtech Kareoke
Wednesday
10:30am illuminatED Panel
12:30 pm Poppin' Tags BYOD


FIGURE 3.2 In this weekly layout, I was super busy, and plotting out the meetings I had to see my available time to better time block tasks really helped.

While this isn't task-oriented, it uses the same principle of blocking out time. In this instance, I have blocked out the units we will study throughout the year and the time I think it will take to accomplish it. Of course, as we know, this isn't ever set in stone and things like lesson plans and yearly plans have to stay fluid—but it does help to think long-term while planning your curriculum.

FIGURE 3.3 A calendex is a combination of a calendar and an index, a way to see how things work in a calendar over time at a glance. You can usually use this method to plan across a bigger span of time, such as months in advance.

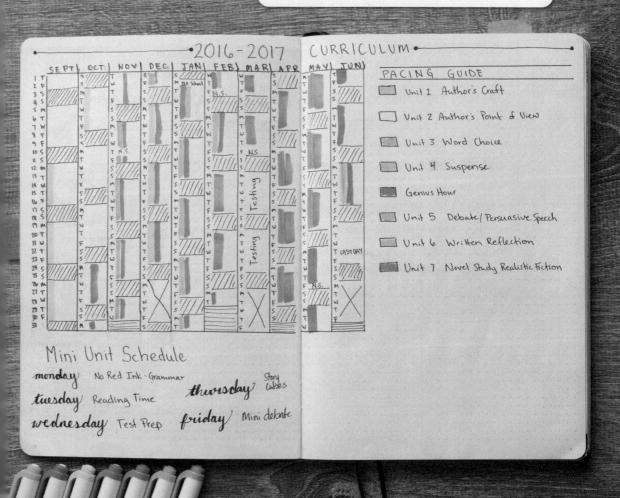

# TIME BLOCKING CHALLENGE

Plan out your week of classes and meetings, and then take a look at your available time and the tasks you have to complete. Try blocking out time for the following things:

- Give yourself some personal time back in the morning and evening. In the morning, try blocking out some "you" time. You could journal, read, do a quick morning workout, or have a cup of coffee while listening to music. In the evening, block out some time to do reflective or gratitude journaling. If there is another project or activity that you would like to do (a creative craft, learning something new, baking something, etc.), block out a twenty- to thirty-minute window just for that purpose.

- Work on batching your grading. Do small amounts of grading in a designated time, no more or less, and don't bring that work home. Do it during contract hours.

- Pick an item that needs to get done around the house and block out time for it. One of my personal favorites to do this with is wiping down the kitchen counters at night. I love waking up to a clean kitchen, but it isn't something I prioritize at night. I should, as it lifts my overall mood the next day—I know this, so I need to block the time out. Figure out that one item for you and schedule time to do it, maybe even time the task so you have a realistic time allotted for it during the rest of the week.

## TIME BLOCKING FOR STUDENTS

Similar to how time blocking can benefit adults, this technique can be very helpful for students. As you can see from figure 3.4, a student's school day is very full. For high school students especially, prioritizing their schedules and blocking chunks of time for homework, studying, practice, and work—as well as their social lives—is critical for their success and for understanding how to better use their time.

Some people are able to prioritize and dedicate their time with little or no effort—it's just how their brains work. Others might struggle with these skills but would never think to use a timer or block out time for tasks. Many students could benefit from being shown how to use time blocking to better manage their time.

As students begin time blocking their days, they will start to notice how full their schedules really are, and how having one point of focus and getting it done in a set period of time can help them complete their tasks efficiently. It can also make planning their weekends helpful and better prepare them to tackle areas of their lives that may once have seemed overwhelming. Again, the goal is not to be so overscheduled that you can't be present in the here and now, but procrastinating and having a ton due all at once doesn't help teenagers either.

### Aesthetic Study Background Playlist

I love listening to music when I need to read or focus. I prefer music without lyrics so that I don't get distracted and sing along. Follow the QR code to see some of my favorite playlists on Spotify and YouTube.

Many parents take over the role of time manager for their kids, but this is such an important life skill that working with students to acknowledge and take control of their schedules will serve them well into the future.

(continues)

  TIME MANAGEMENT

Have students plan out their weeks, looking at available time and tasks. Try blocking out time for the following things:

- In a homeroom/advisory class, have students block out their current schedule, including weekends.
- Have students make note of any upcoming assignments, quizzes, or tests they have in each of their courses.
- Have students create a list of things that motivate them to study and/or what they can reward themselves with when the test is over.

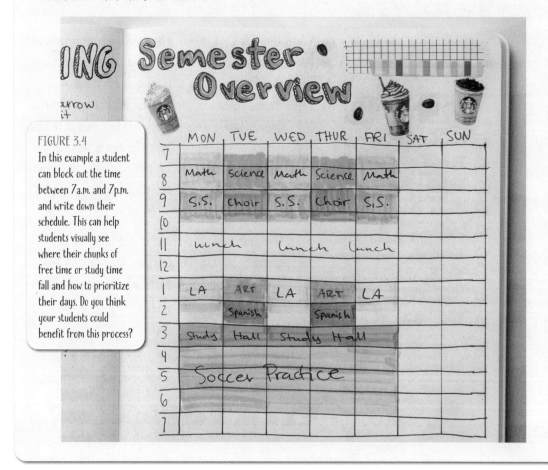

**FIGURE 3.4**
In this example a student can block out the time between 7a.m. and 7p.m. and write down their schedule. This can help students visually see where their chunks of free time or study time fall and how to prioritize their days. Do you think your students could benefit from this process?

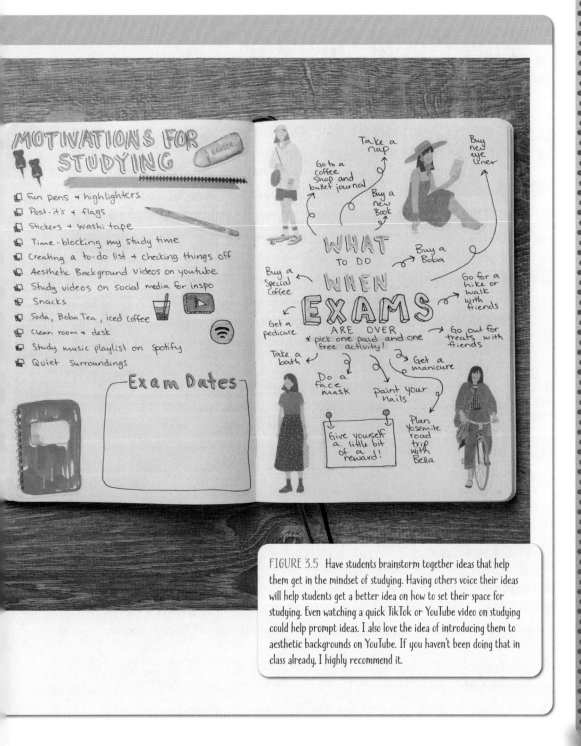

## MOTIVATIONS FOR STUDYING

ERASER

- [ ] Fun pens + highlighters
- [ ] Post-it's + flags
- [ ] Stickers + washi tape
- [ ] Time-blocking my study time
- [ ] Creating a to-do list + checking things off
- [ ] Aesthetic Background videos on youtube
- [ ] Study videos on social media for inspo
- [ ] Snacks
- [ ] Soda, Boba Tea, iced coffee
- [ ] Clean room + desk
- [ ] Study music playlist on Spotify
- [ ] Quiet Surroundings

### Exam Dates

### WHAT TO DO WHEN EXAMS ARE OVER

* pick one paid and one free activity!

- Go to a coffee shop and bullet journal
- Take a nap
- Buy a new Book
- Buy new eye liner
- Buy a Boba
- Buy a Special Coffee
- Go for a hike or walk with friends
- Get a pedicure
- Go out for treats with friends
- Take a bath
- Do a face mask
- Paint your nails
- Get a manicure
- Give yourself a little bit of a reward!
- Plan Yosemite road trip with Bella

FIGURE 3.5 Have students brainstorm together ideas that help them get in the mindset of studying. Having others voice their ideas will help students get a better idea on how to set their space for studying. Even watching a quick TikTok or YouTube video on studying could help prompt ideas. I also love the idea of introducing them to aesthetic backgrounds on YouTube. If you haven't been doing that in class already, I highly recommend it.

# Using Digital Calendars

Something that I have done from the beginning of my career is utilize my digital calendar. One of the first things I did was create a recurring meeting time for every Friday after school to reflect on my weekly lessons. As a new teacher, I thought it would be good to record how things went, what I wanted to change, what I would keep, and so on, so that I could remind myself of what I learned when I would prepare for the next year. This helped me develop a habit of making these recurring notes to myself. I still make them for various things. For example, I have a meeting reminder pop up on my calendar every Wednesday to remind my team that if we need to put anything into the weekly newsletter, it is due by noon! I might sound annoying when I remind my fellow team members, but they often thank me later for the reminder, and we have been consistent as a team at getting out our information to the rest of the staff. I even put a reminder in during a freak snowstorm last year to buy my daughter new winter clothes in October so that we weren't surprised again (or having to buy winter snow pants when everyone else was buying winter snow pants). I thanked myself this year once I got over the cryptic calendar memo of "buy winter clothes for Molly." I make these reminders for everything from working out, to putting the trash out, to newsletter reminders. Without the help of my digital devices, all my little notes and reminders to myself would go missing or disappear into the ether.

# Making the Most of Digital Reminders

Digital tools like Siri and Alexa can help us remember and accomplish tasks. I love using these tools in my home and when I am on the go. Let's talk about how to utilize them to maximize efficiency in and out of the classroom.

According to a study done by Northwestern University in conjunction with Microsoft, digital reminder systems can serve as an aid to help people remember information, especially those things that rely on something called **prospective memory**. Prospective memory is a form of memory that is needed to perform or recall a planned action at a future point in time. These are common in daily life and can range from something super simple like knowing that Tuesday is garbage day, to something more vitally important like remembering to take certain pills at certain times. The use of virtual assistants like Siri, Cortana, and Alexa in our digital devices has become much more popular in recent years, and shows no signs of slowing. The market intelligence firm Tractica, which focuses on emerging technologies, released a report, "Artificial Intelligence Market Forecasts," where they predicted annual global AI software to grow from $10 billion in 2018 to $126 billion by 2025.

I use my phone all the time for quick scheduling reminders, and when I'm at home I use Alexa to remind me of specific things that I need to remember to do. When setting these reminders, it's important that you include a date or time. For example, when I am at work or in the car I might ask Siri to set an alarm on my phone for 3 p.m. to remind me of my next meeting. When I am at home I might ask Alexa to set a reminder for ninety days to remind me to cancel a free trial of a streaming service I just signed up for. Whether setting a reminder for a future event, or a reminder to do something before a future date, automation and AI make the process easier.

## BE JUDICIOUS WITH REMINDERS

Keep in mind that setting too many reminders or even setting them for the wrong time of day can have negative effects. Too many reminders can distract us at work or can even make us feel overwhelmed or bad about ourselves. If your gym emails you a reminder to come work out when you are super busy with work and just can't make it that day, you may end up starting to ignore or even unsubscribe from reminders.

# DIGITAL REMINDER CHALLENGE

First, think about what kind of digital tool you might want to use for reminders. For example:

- Timers on your phone (with Siri on your iPhone or Google Assistant on your Android)

- Digital calendar reminders (with your work calendar system or another like Cozi)

- Reminders at home on devices like Google Home or Alexa

- More advanced "rule" timers like IFTTT

Next, brainstorm a list of some reminders you might like to set now, and then when you develop a system that works for you, set reminders on the spot as you think of them so you don't have to think of it again. Ask yourself these questions:

- **What could you help yourself remember in your everyday life using digital reminder tools?** For example, I have a reminder on my phone at 10:30 a.m., 12:30 p.m., and 2:30 p.m. to drink water, since those are times I will be working and will have my phone near me. At home, my Alexa reminds me on Tuesdays at 5 p.m. to take out the garbage.

- **What could you help yourself remember a month from now?** This could be anything from a birthday to canceling a subscription. This kind of reminder requires you to think about the best time to be reminded. For example, I recently needed to change a subscription for my dog's natural food. Since I am mixing it with dry food, he doesn't eat as much as they think I need, so I needed to cancel the next shipment. I knew I would need a prep time where I had a computer, and I knew it wouldn't take me very long. I found the date the next shipment would be sent, and I backed up a week from there to set my reminder to cancel. The reminder helped me to stop the order before it was shipped.

- **What could you help yourself remember even farther in the future?** My note a year in advance to buy new winter clothes for my daughter before the storms hit was a perfect reminder for me, and now my daughter is ready for a fun snow day.

Digital Reminder Tools

Follow the QR code to see a post about some of my favorite tools for digital reminders.

# Emojis and Color Coding Tips & Tricks

Calendar reminders can look boring, blend together, and if left alone, they can sometimes not highlight when something is more important than something else. One way to avoid this is to visually differentiate reminders by adding color coding or even emojis. Visually separating events in this way can also make a busy calendar look less overwhelming.

When I set up recurring meetings for staff and teams, I use different colors and add emojis to make them stand out. To develop a system I first brainstormed what topics would be most useful to group and separate by color coding, including:

- Meetings
- Trainings
- IEP/504 meetings
- Class periods
- Projects/prep/planning
- Grading time
- Homework (assigning a color to this and tests allows you to visualize when you are starting to assign too much for students)
- Tests
- Important family members

Microsoft recently began sending briefing emails to those using their Enterprise system, with the goal of helping you better sync between your email and your calendar and be more intentional. The system tracks requests, emails from collaborators, documents you might need in a meeting, and suggestions to block out time for things like focus time, taking a break, or catching up on email and messages. It essentially acts as a personal productivity assistant using AI to help you figure out priority communication

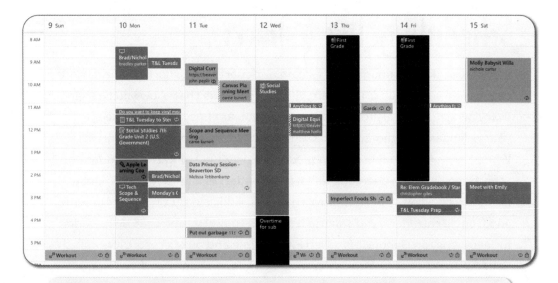

FIGURE 3.6  Coding my digital calendar is helpful for me. I can see that personal things are green, my daughter's appointments are in orange, etc.. What categories would you identify and how would you color code them? How would you use emojis to highlight appointments?

and what needs attention. The email is sent to you because someone in your organization flipped the switch to allow the briefing to go through but you also have the ability to unsubscribe. Google also has a Google Assistant morning briefing. So, AI is using time blocking and color coding too! The more you use these tools as intended, the more you can get out of them.

# Meeting Invitations Tips & Tricks

Another thing I've gotten into the habit of doing is using the description notes for calendar meetings. I add things like links to the notes document we are using, and if it is a virtual meeting, I will add the virtual room link and password to the description. If I am working with a team and we are doing a long-term project, sometimes we get into the habit of leaving notes to ourselves of where we left off at our last meeting so we know where to pick back up.

# Scheduling Tips & Tricks

If you work closely enough with a team or department, sharing your calendar can also be very helpful. There are visibility settings that allow you to share everything in your calendar or show when you are busy. If you are keeping your calendar updated, this is extremely helpful for support staff as well. When trying to schedule meetings for IEPs or 504s, using the calendar and scheduling based on everyone's shared calendars is infinitely better than having to do a ton of back-and-forth emails. Additionally, on both Microsoft and Google calendars, you can use a feature to find a time that best works for everyone (on Google it is called Find a Time and on Microsoft it is called Scheduling Assistant). You can create multiple calendars, so if you wanted to create a calendar for assignments and/or big projects, it is easy to look at each other's calendars when planning to share the load for the students.

# Task Lists Tips & Tricks

Both Microsoft and Google calendar systems also have a to-do list feature that you can use to build reminders with specific dates and times into your calendar. Some may find a digital to-do list more helpful than keeping a to-do list in their handwritten journal. Finding the best approach to work for you is the ultimate goal.

# Technology To Help With Time Management

There are lots of digital tools to help you think about where you have spare or wasted time that you could use more efficiently. There is always time and space to sit down and waste twenty minutes mindlessly scrolling through an app; however, if you are trying to stick to some work boundaries, then making the best use of the time you are given during contract hours is important. Apps like Rescuetime can be useful in helping to track your usage on different websites and apps, which can in turn help you set goals and reflect on your progress toward those goals.

Rescuetime App

When you find you have thirty minutes here or an hour there, you can utilize technology to help stay on task. For instance, another time blocking strategy is called the **Pomodoro technique**, where you give yourself twenty-five minutes to work on something and when that twenty-five minutes is up, you get a five-minute break to do whatever you want. There is a Chrome extension for this technique that will actually block time-sucking sites like Facebook or Pinterest during your twenty-five minutes and then unlock them again during your break.

Pomodoro Extension

We know that the brain needs downtime to recharge and make connections to what we have learned. In the article "For Real Productivity, Less is Really More," published in *Harvard Business Review*, Tony Schwartz mentions that our brains work in ninety-minute rest–activity cycles. Indeed, fifty years ago, sleep researcher Nathaniel Kleitman found that our bodies rest in ninety-minute periods at night. Most people don't talk about this part of the study, but our bodies continue to function in a ninety-minute cycle during the day, too. We go from higher to lower alertness every ninety minutes. This is called our **ultradian rhythm**. While we might be more familiar with the circadian rhythm—the cycle our body goes through in a twenty-four-hour period—this is something that happens in a period shorter than a day but longer than an hour, literally the definition of ultradian. Finding time to rest after at least an hour and a half helps us with productivity. In a very real sense if I am working in the garden, working on a renovation project, or even writing a chapter in a book, there is a certain limit for me on how long I can give all my focus or energy. I have noticed that I will at some point start to get sloppy or make mistakes because I have pushed past an hour or two. I have started to understand the importance of being able to give all of my focus or best effort to a project for a good ninety minutes or so, and then give myself a rest or turn to a different activity. When I don't do this I can easily get frustrated or make a mistake. Utilizing tools that help us track the time and remind us to take breaks is a good thing. It also makes us think differently about how we might lesson plan with students! If we can understand that it is natural for our body to need a break or our mind a rest after a certain amount of time, then we should be paying attention to the student experience not just in terms of content but also in increments of time. To maintain their focus and engagement, and ensure their best output, think about these cycles and how to use them for optimal learning.

Finding time in your schedule to go incommunicado is also valuable. Sometimes the phone ringing and the emails coming into your inbox can be distracting; scheduling yourself focus time for short thirty-minute chunks—where you are solely focused on one task and not answering emails or phone calls—can actually free you up to hit that optimal workflow nirvana. A number of tools can help ensure you can responsibly go offline for a brief period without feeling like you have to check your work notifications. These include things like automatic email responders, switching your phone to "do not disturb" mode, or turning on an automated response about not being available on things like Microsoft Teams.

Switching over to digital submissions from students also helps cut back on grading time. There are built-in technology tools that help you save time; most secondary schools now operate with the use of a learning management system. Get to know the ins and outs of your school's grading program. Using an automatic grade "complete/incomplete" for turn-in is much more efficient than collecting piles of papers for every assignment. We know that offering feedback in a timely manner is essential for student learning. When we take weeks to grade work and pass it back, that feedback is doing a fraction of the good that timelier feedback would be able to do. I have found that by utilizing technology for grading I was able to cut my grading time down to a quarter of what I was doing when I was hauling stacks of papers home. Plus, when I made the switch, my students got more feedback than just a smiley face on their paper.

 # Chapter 3 Key Points

- The idea of time blocking to get our best focus and productivity helps when taking on tasks and mapping out your day. We see evidence of this in research on ultradian rhythm and can use digital calendars and digital assistants with helping keep track of our time spent on different activities.

- Once you understand what works for you in a planner based on a better understanding of your priorities and how you best work with time management and productivity it is easier to find a planner that can work for your specific needs.

- Using different tools to help you be better at time management ultimately comes down to time affluence, becoming richer in how you spend your time on yourself instead of giving your time to someone or something else.

# ISTE Standards Addressed

This chapter addresses several ISTE Standards, including:

## 2.1 Learner

Educators continually improve their practice by learning from and with others and exploring proven and promising practices that leverage technology to improve student learning. Educators:

a. Set professional learning goals to explore and apply pedagogical approaches made possible by technology and reflect on their effectiveness.

## 2.3 Empowering Leader

Leaders create a culture where teachers and learners are empowered to use technology in innovative ways to enrich teaching and learning.

c. Inspire a culture of innovation and collaboration that allows the time and space to explore and experiment with digital tools.

# Reflection

After reading chapter 3, take some time to consider how you will apply some of the strategies to your own life and journal setup.

1. When practicing time blocking, were you able to put in any time for yourself, or were you able to get some time back to yourself?

2. How do you feel about your ability to judge how long a task might take? Is this something you need to work on?

3. How did focusing on being more intentional with your time, aiming toward time affluence, feel while trying some of the challenges in this chapter? Did you see any benefits to your personal or professional life?

# NOTES & DOODLES

# AUGUST

| S | M | T | W | T | F | S |
|---|---|---|---|---|---|---|
| 1 | 2 | 3 | 4 PD | 5 PD 🚚 | 6 🚚 | 7 🚚 |
| 8 🚚 | 9 | 10 | 11 | 12 | 13 | 14 |
| 15 | 16 Mtg | 17 | 18 | 19 🚚 | 20 🚚 | 21 🚚 |
|  |  |  |  | Papa + Nana House Sit → | | |
| 22 | 23 | 24 | 25 | 26 | 27 | 28 |
| 29 | 30 | 31 |  |  |  |  |

## Important Dates

- PD on the Patio
  3-19     KOA 19-22
- House Sit
  18-22
- First Team mtg
  16th @ 8:30 pm

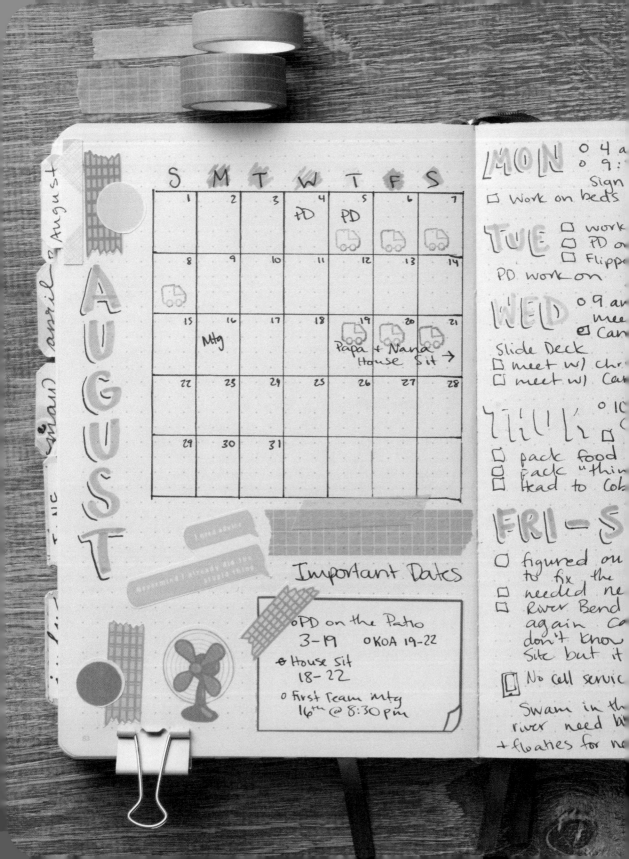

---

**MON**
- 0 4 a
- 0 9:
- Sign
- ☐ Work on beds

**TUE**
- ☐ work
- ☐ PD o
- ☐ Flippe
- PD work on

**WED**
- 0 9 ar
- mee
- ☑ Can
- Slide Deck
- ☐ meet w/ Chr
- ☐ meet w/ Car

**TH...**
- 0 10
- ☐
- ☐ pack food
- ☐☐ pack "thin
- ☐ Head to Col

**FRI - S**
- 0 figured ou
- to fix the
- ☐ needed ne
- ☐ River Bend
  again C
  don't know
  Site but it
- 📱 No cell servic

Swam in th
river need b
+ floaties for n

# CHAPTER 4
# Developing a System That Works for You

## CHAPTER OBJECTIVES

- Answer a quiz to find out what kind of planner is right for you
- Develop a system for planning using monthly, weekly, and daily layouts
- Get comfortable customizing your journal with banners, containers, and doodles
- Understand available online and analog planners and the pros and cons for using them
- Know what to do with premade journals and how to get the most out of them
- Learn how to create digital stickers or customize your own printables

## SUPPLY LIST

- blank journal with dot grid
- stencils
- pens
- highlighters
- ruler

## VOCABULARY

- monthly spreads
- weekly spreads
- daily spreads

# Which Planner Is Right For You?

Answer the following questions to see which type of planner is best for your style, needs, and budget. Use the suggestions to narrow your search.

| QUESTION | ANSWERS |
|---|---|
| What is your budget? | **A.** Minimal |
| | **B.** Willing to spend $20 to $30 |
| | **C.** Willing to spend up to $60 |
| | **D.** Sky's the limit |
| What is your planning style? | **A.** Highly logical |
| | **B.** All the bells and whistles. You are detail oriented and like to "plan all the things!" |
| | **C.** Digital for ease of use and less "stuff" |
| | **D.** Artsy |
| What kind of binding do you want? | **A.** Softcover |
| | **B.** Custom binder or digital |
| | **C.** Spiral bound, hard disc |
| | **D.** Hardcover |
| How do you want your pages set up? | **A.** Yearly or monthly view |
| | **B.** Weekly or daily view |
| | **C.** Monthly or weekly view with reflections/goals |
| | **D.** Blank |
| What size of planner? | **A.** Book-sized or pocket-sized |
| | **B.** Digital planner accessible anywhere |
| | **C.** Large |
| | **D.** A5, normal hardcover size |
| Colorful or minimal? | **A.** Minimal decorations |
| | **B.** Customizable, or a mix of blank and colorful elements |
| | **C.** Colorfully decorated |
| | **D.** Blank, so I can create my masterpiece! |

**If you chose mostly A's: Minimal-ista**

You might do best with a simple, premade planner that you can find at an office supply store or bookstore.

You could also try out dot journaling with any book or notebook you have lying around—yes, even in a cheap spiral notebook! For blank journals that are conveniently sized, look into Field Notes or, from my hometown of Portland, Oregon, I love Scout Books!

**If you chose mostly B's: Digital Diva**

You might like a digital planner from Teachers Pay Teachers, or a hybrid version, like the Rocketbook Panda Planner.

You could look into creating your own using Google slides, especially if you have a touch screen device and a stylus.

You might be interested in a website service like Planner.com where you just type in your information for your daily lesson plans.

You could also look into what your digital calendar systems in Google, Outlook, or Cozi.com might be able to offer you to keep your appointments and other to-do list items easily accessible from any device.

**If You Chose Mostly C's: Pre-made Planner Pro**

You might be looking at Erin Condren, Happy Planner, or a refillable notebook. The refillables (depending on if you get a leather version with all the different inserts) can start to really add up. While the Happy Planner is usually around $20, the add-ins and inserts can start to pile up too. Teacher Happy Planners are more than $30 at a starting point too.

You might be interested in a digital journal that can be found on Etsy or Teachers Pay Teachers. Some Teachers Pay Teachers purchases give you access to the files year after year.

You might be interested in an A5 ring binder or a refillable notebook. Or, you could look at the Rocketbook Panda Planner as a mix between analog and digital.

**If You Chose Mostly D's:** Creativity Designer

You could look into a blank dotted grid journal, or even journals like ban.do journals that are hardbound with layouts and tabs and colorful quotes. Often journals like this can also be found at bookstores too.

You might be looking for an A4 journal. I have a soft cover A4 from Leuchtturm1917 that works as a nice teacher planner. I also classify Erin Condren and Happy Planners from Jo-Ann Stores as fitting in the medium/large category.

You could look into creating your own using google slides, especially if you have a touch screen device and a stylus.

Instead of the Rocketbook Panda Planner, you might be interested in using a normal Rocketbook. Once you find a layout you like you can use a sharpie to create permanent lines and then you can use their Frixion pens that wipe off to reuse over and over again.

n chapters 1 and 2, we talked about filtering. We have so many thoughts throughout the day that it can be hard to keep track of them. This is where developing a system that works for you comes into play. Writing down those important dates, thoughts on projects, to-do lists, and then filtering those from a yearly to monthly to weekly to daily perspective will help you with prioritizing and ultimately being more productive. In chapter 1, we also talked about a future log, where you put the important dates for the long term. The next part of the process is filtering down and looking at each specific month, transferring the important dates from the future log, and then adding those to either your weekly or daily spreads. Let's take a closer look at monthly, weekly, and daily layouts and their piece in this whole puzzle.

# Monthly Spreads

A monthly layout helps you see things at a glance. Spatially, it helps you see things more easily, which can make it easier to plan the weeks and projects during the month. Teachers often use a monthly calendar when lesson planning to think about the broad strokes of the unit within the year, and then we dive into weekly and daily plans.

This is the same concept, but with our daily lives instead of lesson planning. There are so many different versions of what to do for a monthly layout. You could be super minimalistic and just do a list of important dates, you could draw a calendar-style layout (these could take up a two-page spread, or they could take just a portion of one page). Another reason I like this system is because you can play around with different designs and figure out what works for you specifically

**Quick and Easy Layouts with Stencils**

This QR code leads to a fairly large stencil pack but there are smaller ones for a lower price. I love anything that gives me a quick layout for journaling—trace the boxes and you are done!

instead of using what's been determined already by a premade planner. You can choose to add sidebars for goals or big tasks that need to be done that week. You can use color coded symbols to represent different family members or categories; you can also do monthly habit trackers. Another quick tip is to use stencils. I am not a huge fan of stencils for drawing banners or icons but I love them for drawing quick boxes and calendar layouts. Scan the QR code to see one of my favorite sets.

This style of monthly spread is quick and easy, and allows you enough space to include details about your dates and events. You can pair a one-page calendar layout and a one-page date list style, which I have done in figure 4.1. This is a simple layout, and takes just a few minutes to create. You can also run the dates down the center of the page and use one side for professional events and the other side for personal ones (see figure 4.2). To use both

FIGURE 4.1  I find that the monthly spread changes depending on my time frame, how much time I want to spend in creating it and if it is a busy month and I need to pay close attention to dates.

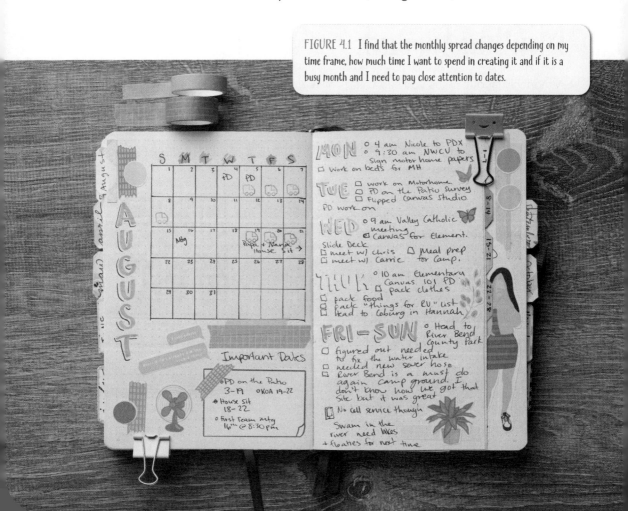

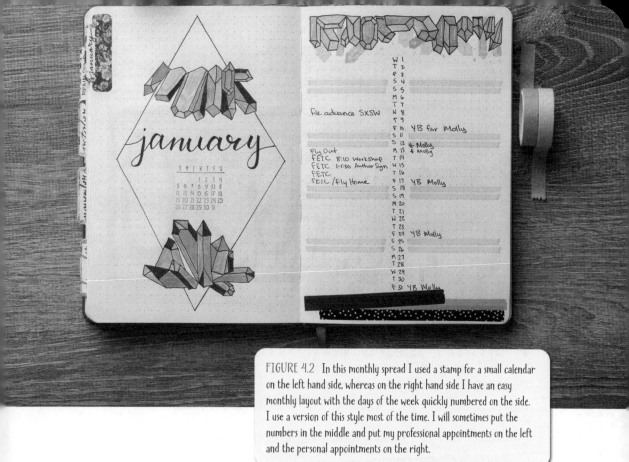

FIGURE 4.2  In this monthly spread I used a stamp for a small calendar on the left hand side, whereas on the right hand side I have an easy monthly layout with the days of the week quickly numbered on the side. I use a version of this style most of the time. I will sometimes put the numbers in the middle and put my professional appointments on the left and the personal appointments on the right.

of these spreads, you need to fill in your dates. I will usually do this by flipping back and forth to my future log. I even have a spread just for family birthdays that I will reference each month. Usually, I also have my digital work calendar open to check dates for the month—but most of the long-term important dates are already in my future log, such as doctor appointments, conferences, flights, and vacations. Another tip is to open up your school district's yearly calendar and either print out a copy and paste it into your journal somewhere (I have done this and it usually goes in the very back), or copy the no-school days, grading days, holidays, and breaks into your future log. I also use a highlighter for the weekends so they stand out. Don't forget you can use different colors and symbols to categorize different events. Stickers and small stamps can also be helpful on these pages.

# MONTHLY SPREAD CHALLENGE

Get out your journal, your pencil and eraser, a ruler, some fineliner pens, or maybe some markers. It's time to create a monthly spread!

- Sketch out your header for the name of the month either at the top or bottom of your page(s).
    - ◆ Think about if you want to add any sidebars for goals, notes, trackers, or doodles.
- Sketch out your calendar.
    - ◆ If you are doing a two-page spread, you can easily fit four or five columns on the left-hand side and two or three on the right.
    - ◆ If you are doing a one-page spread, your boxes will be a lot smaller and your page usually includes a table with seven columns and five rows.

- If you are doing a list view, write the month at the top and then write the dates for the month, starting two "dots" in from the left of the page. Keep in mind I am using either my year at a glance page or my future log to check how many days in the month and which day of the week the first falls on. Once I know the day of the week the first falls on, I will start next to my "1" on that day and write down the first letter of the day next to the number in the first dot column.
- Write out the titles of your sidebars.
- If you have been sketching in pencil first, go back over with your fineliner black pen and add any color, doodles, or stickers you want!
- Fill in your tasks and events on the page, making sure to flip back to your future log and include your important dates.

**Tips for Monthly Spreads**

- I find that having a theme helps when doing my monthly sections. A theme could involve colors I am going to use, or the types of images or doodles I'll include. Colors of washi tape will usually match my marker colors. So for example in the month of march I typically use green marker colors as my highlights, and I will find images or washi tape that also has green tones in it. I find having a theme helps center the work, and I no longer think about the components because I usually gather them when I sit down to do the monthly layout.
- I love to look on Pinterest for images for my journal that fit my chosen theme. Magazine images and art books are also helpful.

For a select few students, organizing and prioritizing their time comes naturally; for all other students, it is a skill that needs to be taught. Here are some ideas to help students with time management, especially those that struggle in general with organization. These strategies can benefit teachers as well, especially when working in teams where it may help to track due dates and projects that might overlap.

## PLAN AHEAD.

At the beginning of each year or semester for older students, and at the beginning of a unit with younger students, it is important that students plan ahead in their planner or calendar (this could be a paper planner or on their digital calendar). Using color coding here would be helpful, such as writing down deadlines in red. If they know ahead of time when a test might be happening they could write that down in green, and then plan for study time ahead of the test in blue. When they do this ahead of time, they will be able to see when they have extremely busy weeks coming and can better prepare.

- For older students, things like class times, sports or band practice times, and work shifts are also important to include, and should be updated regularly.

## ENCOURAGE STUDENTS TO MAKE TO-DO LISTS.

You can download the following printables to print and share with students. Additionally, look into Canva. It's free for educators and there are a ton of templates for to-do lists you can adapt.

## TEACH PRIORITIZATION OF TASKS.

Have students look at their to-do list and develop a system for knowing when something needs to be done today, would be good to finish today, or could be worked on tomorrow. Such a prioritization system could look like a numbered or alphabetized list, or students could come up with symbols (circles, squares, and triangles, for instance) to show what level of urgency a particular task requires. I personally like to use squares for all of my to-do list items so that I can put a check in the ones I finish and an arrow in the boxes that need to be moved to the next day. If a to-do list is really long or convoluted, a student may need to

To-Do List Printables

add numbers to further break down their list of items, or they could highlight particularly essential things that need to get done that day.

## GET STUDENTS TO FOCUS ON ONE CLASS A TIME.

This helps with accomplishing set tasks and not getting lost in multitasking behavior. As we have talked about already, multitasking can make us think we are getting stuff done because we're doing a lot at once, when we're actually not concentrating enough on any one thing to complete tasks properly. So focusing on one area at a time will help with organization.

## REMIND STUDENTS THAT IT IS OKAY TO TAKE BREAKS.

If they are steadily working through their to-do lists and getting things done, taking breaks is good for the brain. A Pomodoro timer works wonders with students. Spend the first twenty-five minutes on task, and then take a five-minute break. They need to stay focused on that timer and not get distracted when they take their breaks. You can easily think you only spent five minutes on TikTok, only to find you have been swiping for half an hour! Teach students that adults have this problem too, and that the ability to regulate social media time is a huge skill to have.

FIGURE 4.3  To-Do List Printable: This easy to print out, letter-sized list has plenty of space for students to brainstorm their ideas.

FIGURE 4.4  For this printable, line up sticky notes in the designated area and run the printed page through your printer again to print on top of the sticky notes. When the page goes through your printer a second time the heading and checkboxes will print on your sticky notes.

# Weekly Spreads

Now, I have to confess that I don't use weekly layouts or dashboards all that often; when it comes to developing a system that works for you, this is exactly what I mean. I personally don't find them necessary in my planning, but that could be different for you! It all depends on how you might be tracking or planning throughout your week, and what ends up being useful. Beyond your monthly spreads, keeping a weekly spread allows you a place to track your habits or goals by week instead of by month. It allows you to describe information from your monthly spread in even more detail, if you feel like that is helpful, and it is a page to dump information throughout the week (without cluttering your monthly spread). A weekly dashboard is a great

FIGURE 4.5  In this example, you can see a simple meal planner box in the top right corner and my big meetings in a box in the bottom left.

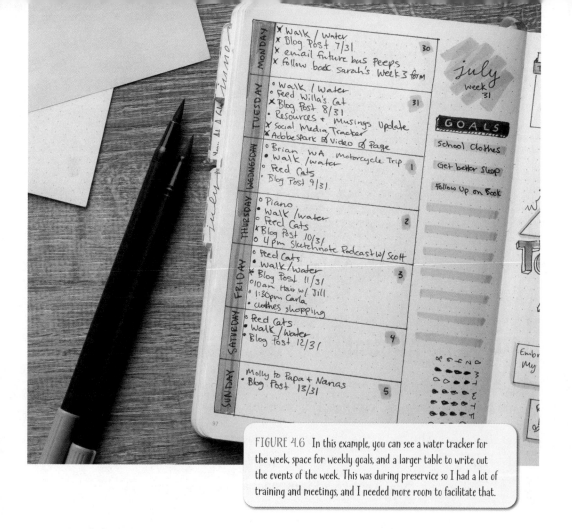

MONDAY
- ✗ Walk / Water
- ✗ Blog Post 7/31
- ✗ email future bus peeps
- ✗ follow back sarah's Week 3 form          30

TUESDAY
- • Walk / Water
- • Feed Willa's Cat
- ✗ Blog Post 8/31          31
- • Resources + Musings Update
- ✗ Social Media Tracker
- ✗ Adobe Spark ☑ Video ☑ Page

WEDNESDAY
- • Brian  WA  Motorcycle Trip
- • Walk /water          1
- • Feed Cats
- • Blog Post 9/31

THURSDAY
- • Piano
- • Walk /water
- • Feed Cats          2
- ✗ Blog Post 10/31
- • 4pm Sketchnote Podcast w/ Scott

FRIDAY
- • Feed Cats
- • Walk /water
- ✗ Blog Post 11/31          3
- • 10am Hair w/ Jill
- • 1:30pm Carla
- • clothes shopping

SATURDAY
- • Feed Cats
- • Walk /water
- • Blog Post 12/31          4

SUNDAY
- • Molly to Papa + Nanas
- • Blog Post 13/31          5

july Week 31

GOALS
- School Clothes
- Get better sleep
- follow up on Book

FIGURE 4.6 In this example, you can see a water tracker for the week, space for weekly goals, and a larger table to write out the events of the week. This was during preservice so I had a lot of training and meetings, and I needed more room to facilitate that.

way to look at patterns in your habits. I have tracked my habits on a monthly spread, and while it is pretty time-consuming to set up, once it is done, it is done for the whole month. Visually, it is a little easier to see those patterns on a monthly level. Think of a weekly dashboard as a place to put your to-do list tasks that aren't assigned to any specific date, but are something you would like to accomplish that week. One thing I love doing on a weekly dashboard is simple meal planning for the upcoming week. While I love cooking, meal planning and shopping are some of the chores that I hate to do. When I don't have my meals planned out for the week, I am more likely to make poor decisions and eat out. Sometimes on my weekly dashboard I will also include a mini calendar of the month.

# WEEKLY DASHBOARD LAYOUT CHALLENGE

Get out your journal, your pencil and eraser, a ruler, some fineliner pens, maybe some markers. Let's practice creating a weekly dashboard together!

- Decide on the components of your weekly dashboard. If you are going to have a header and or a mini calendar, feel free to add that here.

- Think about if you want to add any sidebars for goals, notes, trackers, or doodles.

- Sketch out your layout and think about what you might add: doodles, pictures, stickers, or washi tape.

- Write out the titles of your sidebars and/or boxes.

THIS WEEK

- If you have been sketching in pencil first, go back over with your fineliner black pen and add any color, doodles, or stickers you want!

- Fill in your tasks and events specific to this week on the page, making sure to flip back to your monthly spread, to include your important dates. Filter! As mentioned before, this one of the best things about journaling— looking from big picture to smaller picture, filtering through all your big to-do lists and making it all more manageable.

**Tips for Creating Weekly Spreads**

- I usually have figured out my theme and color palette when doing my monthly layout, so I just continue with that theme. You might prefer using a black pen, which is fine. Do whatever works for you!

- Ask yourself what might be helpful to look at for the week? Is it habit trackers? I find more success when tracking by week than by month actually for most of my habits except water, I track that daily.

- Another option for a weekly layout might be including bigger meetings or events that stretch over what is in the daily sections, just a place to call out what is going on that week beyond your classroom or day-to-day life.

- Another one that I like to include on my weekly spreads is a meal planner box. This is helpful to try and think about my upcoming days, which might be busy and hectic and therefore better for a quick meal or takeout, or which nights I might feel more up to making a meal at home.

# Daily Spreads

The daily spread is by far the most important one for me because this is where I keep track of my daily to-do list. It is also the spread that changes the most for me depending on how busy I might be that week. For example, during the school year I usually need a full page for a single day so that I have plenty of room to write down any appointments or meetings, as well as the things I need to get done throughout the day. Depending on how you are using your bullet journal, this could be where you get to some nitty-gritty with lesson planning: reminding yourself of time stamps on a YouTube video you will be sharing, the number of homework copies you need, or the pieces that still need to be added to your digital lesson on your learning management platform. Additionally, this is where I remind myself of my migrated tasks from the previous day or week, as well as spur-of-the-moment things that might pop up in a team or department meeting. During the school year, having the week set up ahead of time allows me to see on Monday that on Thursday, I will need to text my dad to ask how his doctor's appointment went, or that it is Melissa's birthday.

When I provide myself with the space for a full page per day, I sometimes end up with empty, unused space—and that is where the creativity comes in. Sometimes I like to add a doodle or write a little journal reflection. Other times, I go onto Instagram and look up a lettering challenge. A lettering challenge is often a post with words or phrases curated by a group of people on Instagram that like to practice different lettering fonts. They are often themed for the month, and you can even click on the hashtag for that particular challenge and see how people are

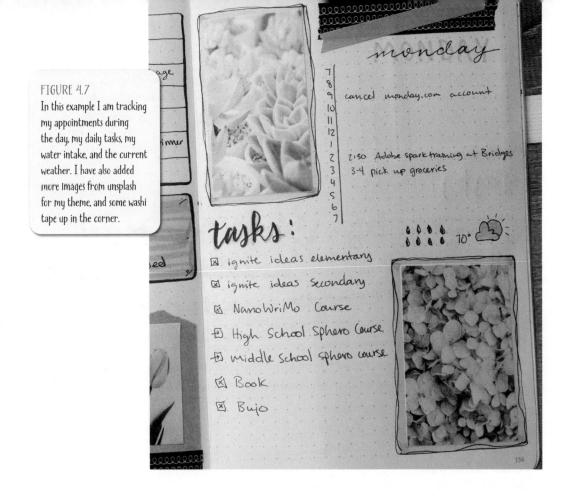

FIGURE 4.7
In this example I am tracking my appointments during the day, my daily tasks, my water intake, and the current weather. I have also added more images from unsplash for my theme, and some washi tape up in the corner.

monday

7
8
9   cancel monday.com account
10
11
12
1
2   2:30 Adobe spark training at Bridges
3   3-4 pick up groceries
4
5
6
7

tasks:

- ☒ ignite ideas elementary
- ☒ ignite ideas secondary
- ☒ NanoWriMo Course
- ☒ High School Sphero Course
- ☒ middle school sphero course
- ☒ Book
- ☒ Bujo

70°

156

interpreting the words and phrases to help you practice. One of my favorite lettering challenge accounts to follow is @letteringchallengehq because they gather and post all the challenges for the month, so it's convenient to just check one space for inspiration. I also sometimes like to fill the blank space with stickers, washi tape, scraps of craft paper or cardstock. I even print out pictures that color coordinate or otherwise fit into the aesthetic of my monthly theme, like coffee and books for November, decorated fireplaces for December, or blooming flowers for May. Search Pinterest for your desired theme and add the word "aesthetic" after; this will usually give you great results.

These pages are for you to practice different elements that can be customized and added to your journals. I've included some examples and prompts, but this is ultimately a space for you to play!

## Banners and Containers

Containers are a way to draw my eye to important details. It is so easy to draw a quick box and fill it with information, or alternatively, write down my information and draw a box around it later.

# Fonts and Lettering

## INLINE PARTS + PIECES

## FANCY 3D PUZZLE TWO Outline

## Script Stich SKETCH Kinder

I have found that including some fun flourishes in my handwriting and use of different pens can add a lot to a page and help me be creative. I tend to use highlighters and my fineliner black pen for this, and they are quick and easy to do.

## Doodles

DEVELOPING A SYSTEM THAT WORKS FOR YOU

# How to Approach Premade Planners

One of the reasons for using a dot journal, which is blank when I start, is that I can customize it to fit my needs. I have had instances before where I was given a small planner by my teacher's union that had all the months mapped out in a nice, pocket-sized planner, and while it was free, it was too small. I would buy a pricey August-to-August calendar simply because it was marketed to teachers, even though it was a premade softcover that didn't fit all my needs. Then there are the super expensive planners that come with all the trademarked products—I have fallen victim to this marketing tool as well. When I spend a lot of money on a product but feel limited by it (e.g., confined to layouts that don't work), I feel guilty when I miss a week or a month of using it. The guilt compounds, and I stop using it altogether because I have all these unused pages that are just sitting there.

In teaching, some weeks are more full with meetings and things you have to do, and others are quick and fly by. I need to be able to use a planner that fits my needs, even as they shift and change. I think the important thing to remember is that there isn't a perfect planner out there, and you have to find a system that will work for you.

If you already have a planner that is working for you, stick with it. You can still take bits and pieces from this book to inspire you to try new ideas. The last thing you need is to have FOMO (fear of missing out) about something that is meant to relieve stress and anxiety. If anything, the prompts and challenges in this book are here to help you reflect, get creative, and hopefully be more productive.

Let's talk about some ideas to work with a premade planner specifically. As I've said before, make it a habit to sit down and work on your planner. Depending on the style of planner you get, this might be something that you do at the beginning of the month, or it could be a daily activity. You will find more success with productivity if you make this as consistent as possible and make your to-do lists earlier in the day so you can prioritize your time. This doesn't have to be a long time; it could be anywhere from five to ten minutes every day or ten to twenty minutes once a week or month. I personally prefer planners that have a monthly section and one that starts at the beginning of the weekly or daily section instead of stacking them at the beginning of the planner away from the other days. Additionally, I think you will find that keeping multiple planners is *more* challenging. I have had people ask me if I keep a separate planner for work and for family; while that is a personal preference, if you are finding it hard to stick to and use a planner, using more than one planner is likely to cause more issues than fewer. It could be as simple as cutting a monthly page in half with a line, one side for work and the other for personal appointments. (I do this with my monthly layouts quite often.) Another option is to use one color of pen for work and another for family. On my digital work calendar, I use the color orange to block out anything for my daughter Molly, and anything that is personal for me is a bright green color.

Be as precise as you can in your calendar. Something that can become an issue is to write in such shorthand that, when you come back to it, you have no idea what it means. In my example about buying winter clothes for Molly, I wrote in January of the previous year for October: "Buy Molly winter clothes." If I had just written "winter clothes," I am not sure if I would have been able to remember what the heck I was thinking when I put that in my calendar. Don't set yourself up for failure by being too vague.

Something to keep in mind when buying any kind of planner is the size, and think ahead to what you'll need it for. You need to take your planner with you most places; if you buy something that is too big and won't fit in your bag for work or purse, then you are more likely to accidentally leave it places. Some of the premade planners are quite large; again, one of the reasons I like dot journals so much in the A5 size is that they are hardbound and will fit in almost all of my bags and purses. If you leave your planner on your desk at work, you may end up forgetting your daily tasks and other important notes. The more compact the planner is, the more likely you are to carry it around with you and use it.

Don't stress about leaving empty space in your journal! You can decide to leave spaces empty, knowing that some weeks are going to be busier than others; or you can choose to be creative with that space. Doodle an image, fill it in with a sticker or washi tape, or use it to reflect on the day. Ultimately, do what feels good but doesn't burn you out. You don't have to fill it all up, especially if you have times where you don't feel like journaling. Consistency is going to help you build a habit, but if you have days where it just isn't working, then let it go for the day and come back to it tomorrow. Before switching a routine up completely, try using a particular planner and system for a few weeks. If you switch things up too often, it will be harder to find peace with your planner and build those habits.

If you there is a length of time where you aren't using your planner but you find yourself wishing to get back into the habit, think of that time not as a period where you gave up or failed. Instead, reflect on what caused you to step away, and work on fixing that for the future. It's a problem to solve, not something to be ashamed of or walk away from. While I know some might say that they want to keep the use of their planner simple; you should walk a fine line between keeping it simple and keeping it fun and creative.

If you have old planners that you've abandoned, you can still use them in different ways. Break out some stickers and washi tape to cover up the old dates and use those planners for other things, like meal planning, doodling, dream journaling, scrapbooking, or collage. I have a few old planners on my shelf that I am now thinking differently about how I might use them. Recently, I used an old planner as a book journal. I covered up the dates at the tops of the pages with book cover stickers and was able to write my reviews and additional information about the books I read. Never feel down about having purchased a planner that doesn't work for you; there are many uses for it, even if it isn't immediately going to work for you as intended.

## PREMADE PLANNERS FOR STUDENTS

Schools often purchase planners for all students to use. These are usually a pretty big expense in the school's budget, but are often used for copying down what the teacher has on the board. I would love to challenge teachers to take some of the same principals we have discussed and apply them to the planners they use with their students. For example, have students decorate the cover and the first few pages, or encourage them to try color-coding with colored pencils.

You can build planner kits for each classroom table. Fill them with stickers, washi tape, and other materials that can be found at a dollar store or donated.

Scan the QR code to get a form letter to parents asking for materials to help build your planner kits.

Encouraging students to personalize and experiment with their journals can be powerful! My daughter used to come home with her school planner covered in very messy handwriting and no ownership in the planner itself. When I got out some fun stationery and showed her how to personalize it with different colored pens, checklists, and section sections, she started to use the planner more.

Letter to Parents for Creating Planner Table Kits

Scan the QR code for a parent letter printable that was made on Canvas.

# Digital, Online, and Analog Planner Options

There are a couple of different options for digital planners online. I have found that I like Planbook quite a lot. While I did in the end pay the $15 yearly fee to use the pro service, they have a free trial option to see if you like it before you buy it. It involved a lot of typing, but a significant perk was that I could print out the day's lessons for a sub if I needed to. I still found that I liked the idea of looking at a month and quickly planning out my days with paper and pencil better than typing out the nitty-gritty on the online platform.

FIGURE 4.8 Creating a digital planner is time consuming but can be done in Google slides! You just need images and the understanding of how to add hyperlinks to images to jump through the planner. You then download it as a PDF and move it to an iPad note taking app.

Another option is to look for a simple monthly Google Slides or Sheets template for a month or day. Some of my favorite go-tos like SlidesMania, SlidesCarnival, or Slidesgo have templates for teacher planners or digital planners. You can work with them straight in Google Slides or PowerPoint and print them out when you need to.

**Planbook Website**

Scan the QR code to go to the website. Currently there is a thirty-day free trial and then it is $15 a year, which is a reasonable price for the service it provides.

## Editable Planners

Another option is to look into planners that you can edit and then download as a PDF and move to an iPad. There are premade options from places like Teachers Pay Teachers, or you can use some of the planners from SlidesMania. The trick is getting the final layout to meet your needs, saving it as a PDF, and uploading it onto your iPad in an app like GoodNotes or Notability. The links to move you throughout the digital journal will still work. Once you get the hang of this idea, you can create your own planners just by using Google Slides; but if you don't want to spend that kind of time on it, you can easily find digital editable planners on Etsy or TPT.

Additionally, you could edit a template and then print it if you don't have access to an iPad. Once you get the month situated the way you like, just print it out and you are ready to go. Some of these planners also have free updates for life, so for $10 or $15 you can buy the current year and come back the next year to get the updated version, which can be a huge money saver.

There are also some hybrid versions, such as Rocketbook's Panda Planner, that allow you to use their layouts with special pens. Once you have the week filled out and used, you can take a picture and upload it to a Google Drive folder or Dropbox and save it before wiping it clean to use for the next week.

# Some Things to Look For

Some planner layouts break individual days into six or eight periods of time to plan out your day. Others focus more on long-term project planning with typically a month-at-a-glance style and less space to write down any of your minutiae. Depending on your needs, think ahead to determine what you will need space for, such as room to write down all of your plans, page numbers, videos and websites needed to teach, etc. An elementary or secondary teacher with multiple preps will likely need something that gives more space to plan out different subjects or periods for the day. Special ed or ELD teachers might need more of a long-term option for big dates during the school year and to track progress with students.

Look into the special features or collections that the planners might have, such as a gradebook, space for notes, and larger monthly sections where you can plan out staff and IEP meetings. Are there any features that you would like and that would be helpful?

Some planners also might run from January to December instead of August to August, so figure out if that will bug you or not. Some planners allow you to see a week at a glance and then will give you a full two-page spread for each day of the week.

Think about size, durability, and binding. Some planners come with a spiral or discbound option. Most planners come with a simple cardboard softcover that can get worn and torn as it shuffles to work and home and back again.

Factor in aesthetics. While many planners are rather plain, some come with colorful stickers and quote pages. What do you need to help you stay engaged and ultimately be more productive? If you haven't done it yet, try the quiz at the beginning of this chapter for ideas and suggestions of where to look.

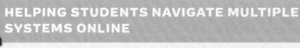

**HELPING STUDENTS NAVIGATE MULTIPLE SYSTEMS ONLINE**

Just like with a physical planner, the most important aspect of using an online calendar is sticking with it and being consistent. In my current district, students can use the calendar in our learning management system, a Google Calendar, and/or the calendar on their phone. Making sure that your learning team, department, or even building is using the same system is key to helping students and parents navigate what and when assignments are due. Usually systems for digital submission of curriculum automatically add assignments to student calendars when you create them, but it's essential to get to know the system. For example, if there is a weeklong project that students should start on Monday and it is due on Friday, it will only show up in their calendar on Friday. So you might have to take the extra step of having students go in and add events or tasks for working on that project the other days of the week.

Additionally, depending on your students' access to a cell phone (or how you feel about having cell phones out in class), you might ask students to pull out their phones and set a reminder about studying for the test that night if it is something immediate. While there are messaging and announcement apps out there for this purpose, the act of having students do this for themselves starts to teach them that this is a valuable skill they can use on their own and outside of school as well. Many adults use their phones for this, but when should students start setting these kinds of reminders? For younger students, we have found great success in adding a label to a shirt at the end of the day with a handwritten or typed note like "Remember to sign parent letter!" instead of setting a reminder on a smart device. How can you encourage students to create their own reminders?

# Using Digital/Editable Printables and Stickers

One thing that I have found to be incredibly helpful and fun with my planners is the ability to make my own stickers. This has been a time saving evolution for me. It started with using stamps to save me time, and then I started working on teaching myself how to make stickers using my iPad and then printing them on sticker paper. If you want to get really fancy, you can look into using a cutting tool like a Cricut, Silhouette, or ScanNCut.

FIGURE 4.9  I loved using this stamp as a shortcut for setting up a new journal! The only requirement is having the stamps and a stamp pad with you, then you can save time by not writing it all out with a pen.

For example, I love being able to create monthly stickers because it cuts down on my time making them in my journal. I remember how much time it took in my very first journal to write out every single month for my year-at-a-glance page, which is usually the first page in all my journals. It took a long time because it was the first planner I had ever set up myself, and I was going slow and trying to make it perfect. I think in that first go, I wrote all the months out in pencil and then went back over it in pen, only to have it pointed out that I had spelled February wrong! After going a couple of years without a fix for painstakingly writing out each of the months, I finally got a stamp (figure 4.9). I really recommend this if creating your own stickers isn't an option; it significantly cuts down on the time I spend on this kind of setup work. The stamp is interchangeable, and also allows you to select if you are starting your weeks on a Sunday or a Monday.

The process of creating stickers isn't as complicated as you think. You can use the Procreate app as I do, or another drawing program that allows for layering. For monthly stickers, you could create a monthly sticker template that is similar to the stamp. You can use the same template for the next year, and just switch the months around. Scan the QR code for a video tutorial on making your own stickers.

Using this kind of drawing app allows you to create all sorts of stickers, anything from the days of the week to creating fun doodles or habit trackers. From there you could just print directly to printer-ready sticker paper. I prefer actual sticker paper to printable label paper, as sticker paper is heavier in weight and is easier to cut. If you do not have a cutting machine like a Cricut, you can cut out your stickers with regular scissors. If you do have a cutting machine, you can either cut away the sticker shape in the drawing app and upload it to the cutting machine app on

### Make Your Own Sticker Tutorial

Follow the QR code and get access to a video tutorial on how I make my own stickers. I also provide access to my reading journal stickers.

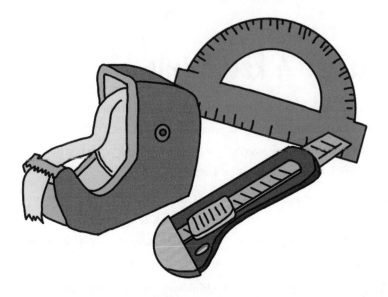

your iPad or laptop for printing and cutting. When I use Procreate, I share the file as a PNG with a transparent background around the stickers to show the machine where I want the stickers cut. Don't worry if that seems clear as mud—my video tutorial explains the process in detail, and includes monthly stickers you are free to download and use!

I have found stickers incredibly helpful in my reading journal. This year I started a reading journal to see if I would like it, and I *love* it! I have stickers to help me with my 1–4 star rating scale, and others to help with book reviews where I ask questions about the quality of writing, ease of reading, pace, quality of content/topic, etc. I was handwriting these in each book but it took a lot of time. I thought the stickers would be easier and save me time; and boy, do they!

Dot journaling people on social media often share freebies that you can use for your planner, so be on the lookout for those. You can often buy printable PDFs of stickers on Etsy or Creative Market as well. Once you buy the PDF, you can print the same stickers over and over again, which I have done. Stickers like this could be a great way to easily do journaling in the classroom as well. You could have stickers for goal setting and tracking that students could add to their spirals or student planners.

# Chapter 4 Key Points

- The main component of developing a system that works for you is to create layouts for the month, week, and day that match your schedule and style. With a blank journal you have the ability to try lots of different styles in order to meet your needs.

- Exploring your line between a functional planner and a creativity outlet means looking at adding doodles, stickers, and washi tape where it makes sense and makes you happy. If you would rather keep things simple and just use a journal and a pen, have at it. It's your journal!

- Something to keep in mind if a blank journal isn't your style is all the planner options that are available on the market; from digital to analog and everything in between. The first step toward getting your money's worth is understanding what will work for you.

- If you have access to a touchscreen device, a stylus, and a printer, you can delve into the world of making your own customized stickers. This is something that has allowed me to tap into my creative side and continue to personalize my journals.

 # ISTE Standards Addressed

This chapter addresses several ISTE Standards for Educators, including:

**2.1 Learner**

Educators continually improve their practice by learning from and with others and exploring proven and promising practices that leverage technology to improve student learning. Educators:

a. Set professional learning goals to explore and apply pedagogical approaches made possible by technology and reflect on their effectiveness.

### 2.3 Empowering Leader

Leaders create a culture where teachers and learners are empowered to use technology in innovative ways to enrich teaching and learning.

c. Inspire a culture of innovation and collaboration that allows the time and space to explore and experiment with digital tools.

 Reflection

After reading chapter 4, take some time to consider how you will apply some of the strategies to your own life and journal setup.

- Thinking about what you learned about monthly, weekly, and daily spreads, how do you see these working their way into your journaling sessions? What will you use, or what have you tried up to this point?

- Looking at the I Do, You Do sections (mini calendar, banners and containers, fonts, and planner doodles), what did you find fun to do and what was challenging? Can you see any of these pieces working in your journal?

- Do you think you will use journaling and goal setting techniques with your students?

- What is your budget for using journals and planners? How can you stick to that budget and plan accordingly?

- How did the "Choose the Right Planner for You" quiz help in your understanding of finding the right planner for your needs?

# Coloring Page

CHAPTER 5

# Journaling Strategies for Managing Mental Health

## CHAPTER OBJECTIVES

- Discover the mental benefits of doodling and attempt to add more doodling to your journaling practice
- Understand the benefits of gratitude journaling and how to find the right balance of gratitude versus searching for positivity when something isn't there—which crosses the line into not being helpful
- Learn some strategies for both yourself and students that have ADHD
- Learn some strategies for yourself or students that are diagnosed with autism
- Know about mental load and how you can help manage stress by making the invisible tasks visible
- Be prepared to build a positive support system at school to help with your work/life balance

## SUPPLY LIST

- journal of your choice
- pens, highlighters, other journaling supplies
- stickers or washi tape

## VOCABULARY

- collection pages
- gratitude journaling
- interoception
- line a day
- mental load
- second shift
- zentangles

A s I have previously shared, when I have blank space in my journal, I sometimes fill it in by doodling. Part of the reason for this is that when I started my dot journaling journey, I was simultaneously teaching myself to sketchnote—the two are inextricably linked for me. My sketchnoting got better because I was doodling in my journals, and my journals got better because I could use containers from my sketchnotes in my journals. As I added to my visual vocabulary from sketchnoting, those things would find their way into my journal. Sometimes if I am in the middle of a meeting and I have my journal near me to add to my task lists, I might doodle then, too.

## Research and Strategies for Journaling to Help Mental Health

According to a 2016 article on the Harvard Health blog, doodling is a form of fidgeting in some capacity, and often it helps us to stay attentive instead of passive. Doodling can help with focus and concentration as well as retention. The act of writing down your tasks, and adding some doodling on top of that writing, has a whole lot of benefits for our brains. Additionally, the spontaneous doodle can sometimes be a psychological de-stressor, allowing you to have a mental break—especially when you might be having a hard time understanding something. In fact, if you are having a hard time focusing, setting a timer and giving yourself a little time to doodle in your journal can allow the "focus-circuits" in your brain to turn off and your "unfocus-circuits" to turn on, giving yourself a little breather. After a few minutes, you will often find it much easier to re-engage and solve your current problem or area of focus, probably more creatively (Pillay, 2016). As I have mentioned in my previous work on sketchnotes, those that doodle have higher information retention, allowing you to better pay attention and recall information. If you are doodling in your journal alongside your goals and tasks, you are more inclined to meet those goals and remember your tasks.

A 2017 Drexel University study looked at the biological effects of doodling and found that it boosts blood flow to the frontal cortex of the brain, which helps with mood. Essentially, doodling has the psychological benefit of an increased feeling of pleasure or well-being. They also looked at the participants' levels of cortisol, the hormone in the brain associated with stress. The study found that those in the study and that made art had reduced cortisol levels—and it didn't matter if they were artistic or not. Overall the scientists found that one of the biggest implications of the study was that there is "inherent potential for evoking positive emotions through art-making and doodling especially" (Otto, 2017). One of the biggest hinderances to doodling is the negative connotation attached to the act, so if we can re-imagine it and see it as a judgement-free, pleasurable activity there are a lot of really great benefits!

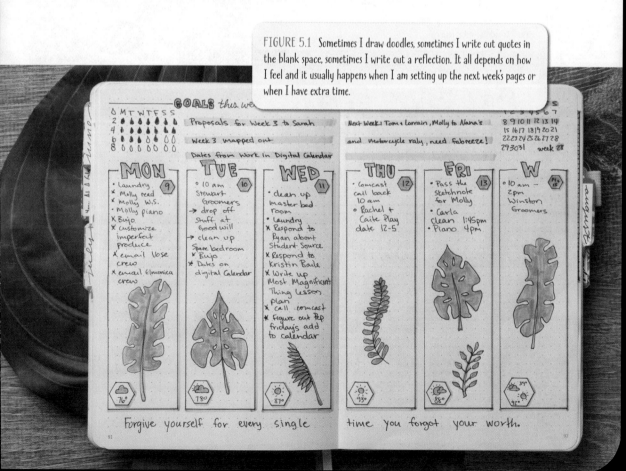

FIGURE 5.1  Sometimes I draw doodles, sometimes I write out quotes in the blank space, sometimes I write out a reflection. It all depends on how I feel and it usually happens when I am setting up the next week's pages or when I have extra time.

Zentangle Doodle for Beginners

One of my favorite activities is to doodle along with people on YouTube, Instagram, or even TikTok. The longer videos on YouTube have an extremely calming effect on me. When I'm teaching about sketchnotes and doodling along with the group, I could be speaking to a room of hundreds of people and not paying attention to time and the stressors of public speaking. Even if I might have previously had a little tremor in my voice from nerves, that goes away once I spend a little bit of time doodling. One way to try this for yourself is by drawing **zentangles** or zen doodles, which are done as a meditative practice to help you achieve calmness or zen. Scan the QR code for a zentangle tutorial on YouTube to give this calming meditation a try.

FIGURE 5.2   I found these stickers at the dollar store and added them into my journal to flip to and color when I wanted to take a quick break. So if you have stickers or if you just draw a page with boxes that you can later fill in with your own zentangle doodles, this is a good mental health spread to add to your journal.

# Benefits of Gratitude Journaling

From time to time, I will include a page in my monthly layout for a **"line a day"** (a one sentence reflection on what happened that day). This originally started when I was trying to keep a gratitude section in my bullet journal, and I quickly realized that I couldn't always identify something to be thankful for. Instead, I found myself writing a quick line about what happened that day. Some months, I'm a lot better at filling in each line; in others, I might only write a handful of sporadic comments. But I keep coming back to it again and again. According to an NPR Morning Edition Your Health story, research shows that those who keep a gratitude journal can have better sleep patterns, lower stress, and improved interpersonal relationships. Interestingly enough, when the study was done with adolescents, they saw a decrease in materialism, a boost in generosity, and even better eating habits (Singh, 2018). Listen to the story by following the QR code.

The positive psychological effects of **gratitude journaling** are so powerful it is an easy piece to add to your journaling practice; however, there is such a thing as finding a balance. Doing it a few times a week can lead to positive results, but trying to do it every day can also lead to negative effects, such as dishonesty or feelings of failure, guilt, or inadequacy if you don't always feel like you have something to be thankful for. This is something I figured out intuitively when I

NPR: "If You Feel Thankful, Write It Down. It's Good for Your Health"

This three-minute news story explores the benefits of daily gratitude.

went from a gratitude journal to just doing a line a day for myself; you may also need to find a balance that works for you. In *Psychology Today*, Amy Morin shares seven scientifically-proven benefits of keeping a list of things you are grateful for in your journal:

1. Opening yourself up to new friendships (showing someone your appreciation can open the door to a new friendship)

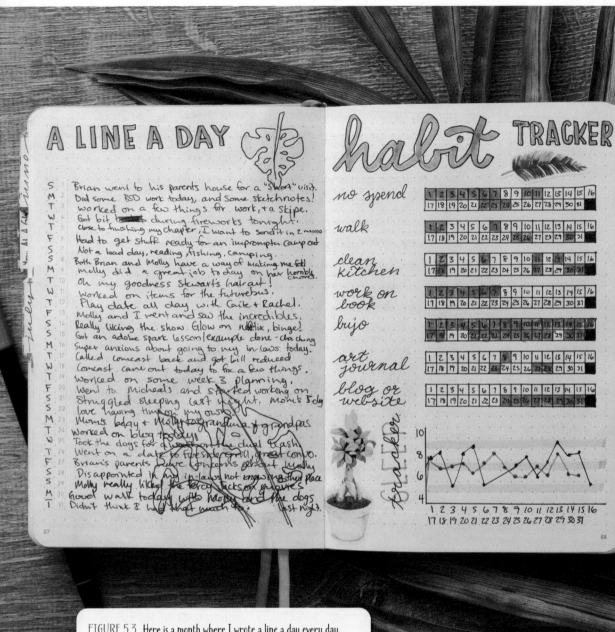

# A LINE A DAY

**habit TRACKER**

S 1 Brian went to his parents house for a "short" visit.
M 2 Did some BSD work today, and some sketchnotes!
T 3 Worked on a few things for work, +a skype.
W 4 Got bit ~~twice~~ during fireworks tonight.
T 5 Close to finishing my chapter, I want to send it in 2 ~~months~~
F 6 Had to get stuff ready for an impromptu camp out
S 7 Not a bad day, reading, fishing, camping.
S 8 Both Brian and Molly have a way of making me ~~f~~
M 9 Molly did a great job today on her horrible chores.
T 10 Oh my goodness Stewart's haircut!
W 11 Worked on items for the futurebus.
T 12 Play date all day with Caite + Rachel.
F 13 Molly and I went and saw the incredibles.
S 14 Really liking the show. Glow on ~~Netflix~~, binge!
S 15 Got an adobe spark lesson/example done - ~~checking~~
M 16 Super anxious about going to my in-laws today.
T 17 Called comcast back and got bill reduced
W 18 Comcast came out today to fix a few things.
T 19 Worked on some week 3 planning.
F 20 Went to Michaels and started working on
S 21 Struggled sleeping last night. Mom's 5dy
S 22 love having them on my own.
M 23 Moms bday + Mother to grandma + grandpas
T 24 Worked on blog today!
W 25 Took the dogs for a ~~walk~~ on the dual trash
T 26 Went on a date to fireside grill, great convo.
F 27 Brian's parents have concerns about Molly
S 28 Disappointed in my in-laws not knowing their place
S 29 Molly really liked the percy jacks on youtube.
M 30 Good walk today with Molly and the dogs
T 31 Didn't think I had that much to ~~say~~. last night.

**no spend**

| 1 | 2 | 3 | 4 | 5 | 6 | 7 | 8 | 9 | 10 | 11 | 12 | 13 | 14 | 15 | 16 |
| 17 | 18 | 19 | 20 | 21 | 22 | 23 | 24 | 25 | 26 | 27 | 28 | 29 | 30 | 31 | |

**walk**

| 1 | 2 | 3 | 4 | 5 | 6 | 7 | 8 | 9 | 10 | 11 | 12 | 13 | 14 | 15 | 16 |
| 17 | 18 | 19 | 20 | 21 | 22 | 23 | 24 | 25 | 26 | 27 | 28 | 29 | 30 | 31 | |

**clean kitchen**

| 1 | 2 | 3 | 4 | 5 | 6 | 7 | 8 | 9 | 10 | 11 | 12 | 13 | 14 | 15 | 16 |
| 17 | 18 | 19 | 20 | 21 | 22 | 23 | 24 | 25 | 26 | 27 | 28 | 29 | 30 | 31 | |

**work on book**

| 1 | 2 | 3 | 4 | 5 | 6 | 7 | 8 | 9 | 10 | 11 | 12 | 13 | 14 | 15 | 16 |
| 17 | 18 | 19 | 20 | 21 | 22 | 23 | 24 | 25 | 26 | 27 | 28 | 29 | 30 | 31 | |

**bujo**

| 1 | 2 | 3 | 4 | 5 | 6 | 7 | 8 | 9 | 10 | 11 | 12 | 13 | 14 | 15 | 16 |
| 17 | 18 | 19 | 20 | 21 | 22 | 23 | 24 | 25 | 26 | 27 | 28 | 29 | 30 | 31 | |

**art journal**

| 1 | 2 | 3 | 4 | 5 | 6 | 7 | 8 | 9 | 10 | 11 | 12 | 13 | 14 | 15 | 16 |
| 17 | 18 | 19 | 20 | 21 | 22 | 23 | 24 | 25 | 26 | 27 | 28 | 29 | 30 | 31 | |

**blog or website**

| 1 | 2 | 3 | 4 | 5 | 6 | 7 | 8 | 9 | 10 | 11 | 12 | 13 | 14 | 15 | 16 |
| 17 | 18 | 19 | 20 | 21 | 22 | 23 | 24 | 25 | 26 | 27 | 28 | 29 | 30 | 31 | |

**tracker**

10

8

6

4

1 2 3 4 5 6 7 8 9 10 11 12 13 14 15 16
17 18 19 20 21 22 23 24 25 26 27 28 29 30 31

67

88

FIGURE 5.3 Here is a month where I wrote a line a day every day.
This is not always the case, and I don't give myself a hard time about it if
I don't keep it up. This is a simple spread that is easy to incorporate into
my journal set up.

2. Better health (people that have things to be thankful for catalog fewer aches and pains)

3. Increased mental health (increases happiness, decreases depression)

4. Enhanced empathy and reduced aggression (thankful people have less reason to seek revenge)

5. Better sleep (especially if you jot down your gratitude right before bed)

6. Better self-esteem (thankful people can see their accomplishments easier)

7. Increased mental strength (thankful people tend to foster resilience in themselves) (2015)

Give this a try in your journal and see what works best for you. Maybe it's a few "I'm grateful for..." boxes on a page that you fill in over the course of the month, or try doing a line a day, sneaking in a line of gratitude when it fits and a line of daily journaling when it doesn't.

# Strategies for Ordering the Chaos and for ADHD

The process of filtering your tasks and thoughts, migrating things that don't get done, can reduce your stress level and improve your work-life balance. Your time is actually finite, and you can't keep migrating twenty to fifty tasks from one month to the next; you either realize it isn't important, or you get it done. If this sounds like you, and if you tend to try new systems and never follow through, I recommend starting with the basics. Try creating an index or table of contents to keep track of where you put things in your journal. Do a list layout of a monthly spread—where you number from one to thirty-one (depending on the month)—and start writing down your big appointments and events, keeping these in shorthand. On the opposite page, you can write in more details if you need to, or start your to-do list. It's really that simple. Start there.

Once you get a simple monthly list integrated into your habits, you can start adding in more things. If you notice you like to keep track of the books you read, add that as a spread (these are called **collection pages**). If you would like to have a doodle page, add that in—just remember to come back to your table of contents or index and write down what page you put things on so you can easily find them later. You have freedom here to find the balance that works for you and that keeps the journal easy to use. Avoid, however, the temptation to go overboard, doodling and decorating at the expense of efficiency (or your time).

Don't hyperfocus on making it perfect, either. I like to remind people to embrace their mistakes; for instance, I was recently setting up my journal for the new month while I was, to be honest, somewhat distracted on a Zoom call. I wanted to get it done so that I could start my daily tasks for the week. I kept coming back to it for the next two days, but I hated the layout and design. When I had more time one evening, I went back in and reworked what I didn't like, gluing some craft paper over the top of a page that was bugging me and writing over the top of it. On another spread, I used watercolor for the first time and realized an hour later that I had numbered the days of the week wrong. I embraced the mistake, slapping some extra paper on from the back of my journal and rewriting the days. Problem solved—not elegantly, perhaps, but usable. More importantly, instead of looking at the mistakes, getting frustrated, and walking away, I just covered them up and kept on going. Sometimes, those imperfections can cause us to not want to use the journal or system but if you can find a way to embrace your mistakes (maybe even get a little creative!), you will find it a great outlet for building resilience.

Another simple idea is to have a designated place and time for your journaling. If carrying it around wherever you go is too much (especially if this might lead to it being misplaced), then think about purposely leaving it at home on your desk, counter, or nightstand. You could also create a journaling station on your couch with a lap table and your favorite pens, and then journal while watching TV alone or with members of your household. Setting a time, such as after dinner for twenty minutes, can also help to make it a habit. Again, start with the simple pieces and then ramp up from there based on what will work for you. If journaling in the morning to set priorities and then journaling again at night for daily reflection and gratitude is too much, then doing just one short attempt once a day is better than none at all.

# Goal Setting for Students with ADHD

Goal setting and prioritizing tasks is an important skill for all students. When schools buy premade journals for students, teachers usually get into the habit of having students write down their daily assignments from the board. Allowing students to decorate their journal or planner and accept ownership is key to starting to develop a positive relationship with the journal. The next is to provide fun markers, colored pencils, and stickers for planner time. See my student challenge later in this chapter for more ideas on putting together table planner kits to help engage students with their journals. But ultimately for students that have ADHD, keeping things simple is the same for them as it is for adults.

People with ADHD need skills like this to help them order the chaos; if they aren't taught this in an academic setting, we are doing them a disservice. It helps them prepare for college, careers, and life in general, so we should make it a priority.

At the beginning of the month, have students identify three things they would like to accomplish. If there is a space in the premade planner's monthly section, put it there, or find another likely spot (they usually have a spot for spelling words or notes) and have them write there. If students are using their own spiral or composition notebooks, you could print out the goal setting printable shared later in this chapter and have them glue that in, or even have them tape it into their premade planners. Have them write down those three goals, then come back and check on those goals one or twice a week. You can continue to write the daily lessons and assignments, but allow them time to check on their goals. Goals can be either academic or personal, think acts of kindness, engagement with family and friends, etc. This could be as simple as saying a compliment to one person a day, doing your chores without complaining, or asking every member of your household about their day. I would highly encourage students to make both types of goals. When they accomplish a goal, they can cross it off their list.

FIGURE 5.4 In this printable you can have students identify those three goals and an action plan.

Goal Setting for Students

Download this printable to use with students for goal setting.

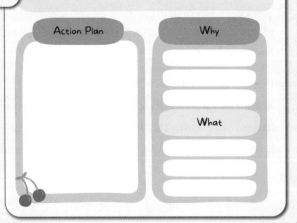

**GOAL SETTING**

Month: _____

Goals

1

2

3

Action Plan

Why

What

# THE VIBE OF THE WEEK IS...

## TOP 3 WINS

## brain dumps

- ☐
- ☐
- ☐
- ☐

## 3 CHALLENGES

## I TE

THIS WEEK...

I WIL

FIGURE 5.5   Here is a simple spread that can easily be drawn in a student's journal to just plot out the week and think about the "vibe" you want to set for the week.

## DOODLING AND STUDENT CREATIVITY

For those students that are prone to losing things there is an added benefit when they have a sense of pride and accomplishment attached to an object, so allowing students to doodle and add their own personality to their journals will help them associate positive feelings with their journal and possibly form more of an attachment to it. There is also a higher probability that those feelings will help with object permanence and make losing the journal a less common occurrence.

Another thing to be aware of is that people with ADHD often lose things. If you have a student that is prone to misplacing things in the classroom—and especially those that have really adapted to the idea of a journal and would be heartbroken if they lost theirs—consider a way to digitally back up their work, or at least their goals. They could create a Google Drive folder and take pictures of their journal pages to upload to that folder. Or if you are using a learning management system, they could take a picture of their monthly goals and upload it as an assignment. One of the benefits of using a classroom app like Seesaw, ClassDojo, Google Classroom, or Canvas is letting families connect with their students' work. Parents would love to know that students are working on goal setting and prioritizing their to-do lists.

# Journaling Strategies for Those with Autism

Autistic people often struggle with time management, listing, and organization. Additionally, they may have issues with executive function, which directly relates to control of behavior in successfully monitoring and attaining chosen goals, attentional control, and working memory. Funneling some energy into the basics of something like journaling can be incredibly helpful for people with autism. **Interoception**, or the ability to sense the internal state of your own body, is another area that can be affected by autism, so adding in purposeful check-ins and reflection could be extremely beneficial. It can be hard for someone to check in on their own body and recognize that they need to get up and move, or get a drink of water. A habit tracker could be the physical representation of a mental check-in. Visual reminders and set days or times in your routine to check your habits can help with that daily part of executive functioning and interoception.

Of course, we know and recognize that autism is on a spectrum, so it is incredibly important to make your journal work for you and your needs. Instead of buying something that is premade and could become a distraction, or more of a pain to use and fill in than it is a help, you can build something that is helpful for your individual neurodivergent needs. Often a student with ADHD or autism is on a 504 plan or an IEP, where you as a teacher need to track habits or accommodations. This could be something that you take care of as a teacher, or a student could track certain habits and goals. This also gives some structure, the opportunity to come back and check in with tasks and goals, and many will thrive with the creative aspect of journaling, too. Bottom line, finding the "why" behind using a journal and setting up a schedule to make journaling a routine are foundational steps for those with autism.

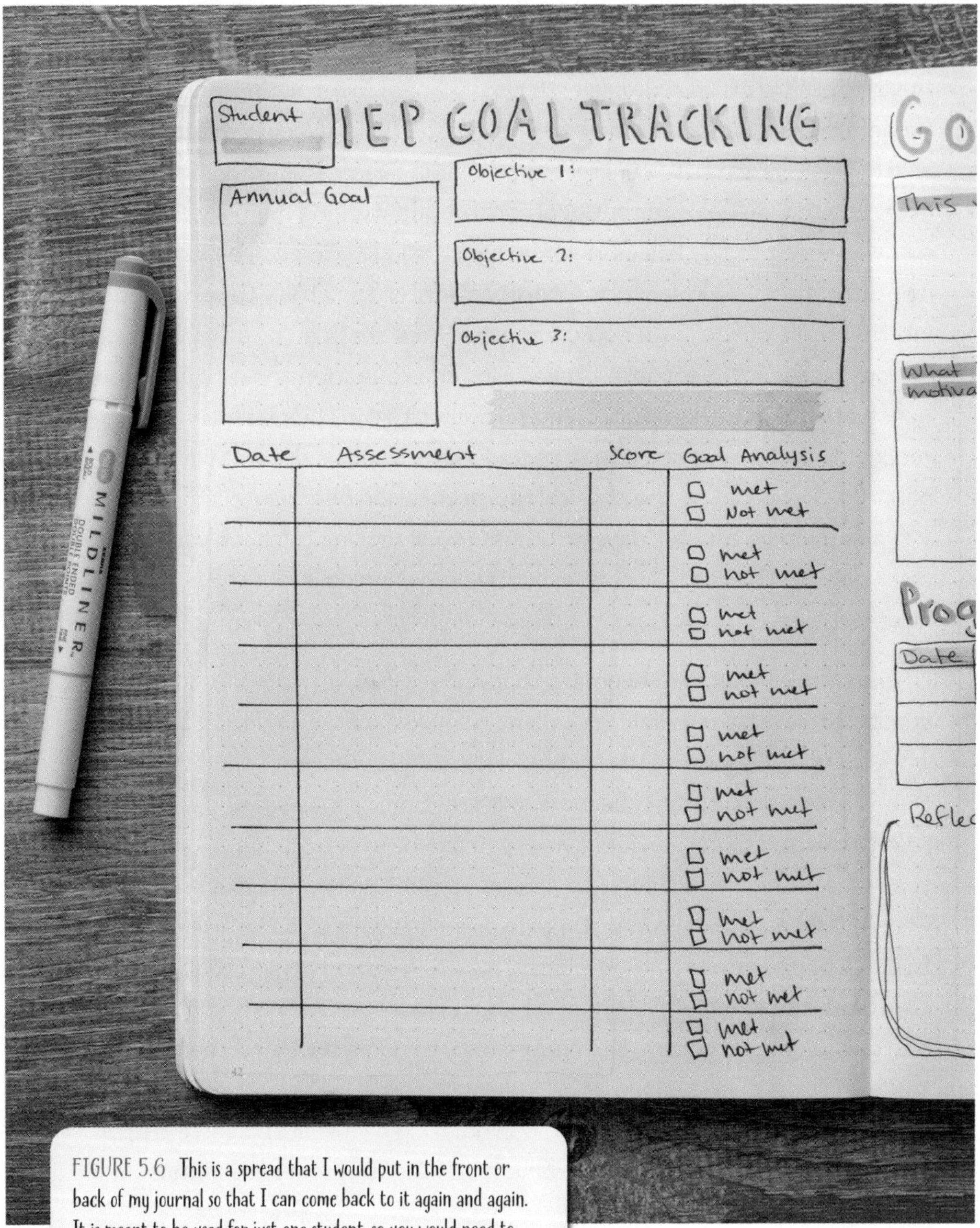

FIGURE 5.6 This is a spread that I would put in the front or back of my journal so that I can come back to it again and again. It is meant to be used for just one student, so you would need to make a version of this for each student on your roster with an IEP or 504.

# Mental Load, Prioritizing Your "Need to Do" to Help Manage Stress

A study conducted by Arizona State University in 2019 and published in the journal *Science Daily* highlighted how invisible labor has a negative impact, particularly on the well-being of women making decisions and running households. **Mental load** is the mental to-do list that women typically keep for their entire household. It is all the little things in your mind, like remembering when to buy more shampoo, and when you need to buy new winter clothes for your youngest because he grew out of them last year. Because these are usually invisible tasks, they might not impact your day-to-day life, but over time they can weigh you down mentally. Mental load and the countless invisible tasks burdening so many of us are often rarely noticed or valued. Add to this the fact that teaching is a woman-dominated field where teachers have to make constant judgements while in the classroom, and then go home to the **"second shift"** to make even more decisions for their family. The second shift is the domestic work you do once you get home from your paid job.

Researchers have identified that those who feel solely responsible for the household and children can experience decreased satisfaction in their lives and partnerships. For those experiencing this, or for anyone who may be feeling overwhelmed, looking at the division of labor—both at work and at home—and asking some of the questions in the following challenge can help address inequalities and identify how to equalize the balance of work.

# MENTAL LOAD CHALLENGE QUESTIONS FOR HOME

The following exercise is meant to help you think about your mental load and the invisible tasks that can weigh you down. Putting those invisible tasks down on paper and then potentially talking to your partner about them can be helpful to not only see all the things that you are unconsciously tracking, but also a way to help create a more equitable division of labor.

**Organizing Family Events**

- List out the family's schedules in your journal or on a piece of paper to go over with your partner. Even if you have a shared family calendar, sometimes it can get lost or be harder to track when seen a month at time.

- List out some of the upcoming events that need to be organized or scheduled, and break up those tasks.

### Fostering Children's Well-Being

- This might take a while, but think about and list some of the things you do during the day to check on and support the physical and mental health of your children.

  - ◆ Do you text your child during the day to make sure they feel okay? Do you make sure to have a snack ready when they get home from the bus? Do you make sure that you have a favorite pair of pajamas clean and ready for them at bedtime?

  - ◆ This activity might take you more than just twenty minutes; in fact, You might make this a spread in your journal that you add to over the next week or so.

- Once you feel like you have added a few items to this list and can start to see some patterns developing, go to your partner and discuss dividing up the load.

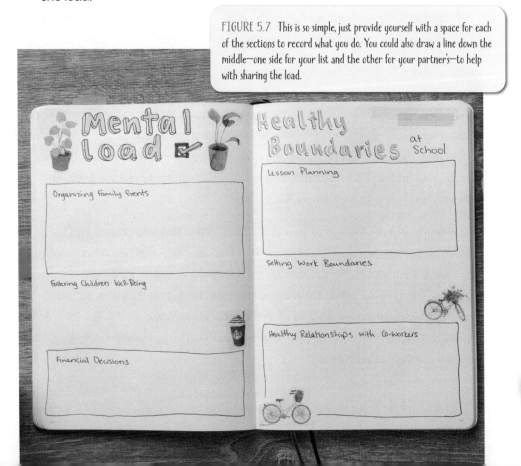

FIGURE 5.7  This is so simple, just provide yourself with a space for each of the sections to record what you do. You could also draw a line down the middle—one side for your list and the other for your partner's—to help with sharing the load.

## Making Major Financial Decisions

A large portion of dissatisfaction at home stems from finances, which can add significantly to your mental load. The following are more general journal prompts to get your brain thinking about this incredibly nuanced topic. You can choose to do this alone or with others in your household. If doing it together, take a piece of paper and fold it in half. Answer the following questions on one side, then turn it over and have your partner answer them on the other. When you've both finished, unfold the paper and look at it together.

- Describe your relationship with money in a few words.
- Describe your relationship with money and your partner in a paragraph.
- What does it mean to you to have "not enough" or "too much" money?
- What is the purpose of money to you? What do you think is the purpose of money to your partner? Go over these answers together and see how much you align and how much you differ.
- How do you feel about money right now, and how would you like to feel about money in the future? How can you both work toward that goal?

There is also a link between invisible labor and feelings of being overwhelmed, and feeling empty within your everyday lives. When you feel supported, you can have emotional resources to cope well with any demands you might face, in the classroom or at home. If you can address where you see inequalities at school or at home, then you create a household or a classroom that is more functional and less burdensome, and spare yourself some mental labor in order to find more time to care for yourself.

The Arizona State study also found that it's incredibly important to find authentic connections with other people that are supportive. When you don't have a support circle, it can be really hard to reduce stress, and you see more burnout at work. On a more granular level, the lack of a support network causes increased levels of the stress hormone cortisol. Recall from the beginning of this chapter, journaling and doodling can help to reduce the levels of cortisol in your brain!

# BUILDING AND MAINTAINING A HEALTHY SUPPORT SYSTEM AT SCHOOL

Similar to the mental load questions for the home, let's take a look at how we can do a better job with our partnerships at work to equalize the load. The following questions are an exercise to help you think about your mental load at work. Putting those invisible tasks down on paper and then potentially talking to your teams or departments can be helpful to not only visualize all the things that you are unconsciously tracking, but also a way to help make a more equitable division of labor on your team.

**Lesson Planning**

- How much of the lesson planning and understanding of the curriculum within the team or department is shared?

- Do you have a team agenda for your meetings? If not, should you start one? This help keep everyone on task and make sure you cover items that you might otherwise forget.

- Go over some of the upcoming units you have and think about how you can divide and conquer as a team. Think about each person's strengths, too. For instance, at the elementary level, if you have one teacher that is particularly good at getting results in math, they should do the math unit. In secondary, if you have a teacher that is particularly good at anchor charts or designing tests, they should be working on that.

In my experience, the teams that worked together had less stress and more engagement with their lessons—and this was even more prevalent during distance learning at the height of the COVID-19 pandemic.

**Setting Work Boundaries**

- What are your current work boundaries? What limits have you set for yourself to protect your own well-being?

- In an effort to shut off your mental load for the classroom, work on developing some rules and boundaries for yourself. Logistically, for example, my contract hours were from 7:15 a.m. to 3:15 p.m. I did not do that much prior to student arrivals in the morning, but that was mostly when we had meetings. I would try and get my copies and other small tasks done before leaving each day. I am not a morning person, so I would try and be as productive during my planning period as I could, and I would leave the building at 4 p.m. every day. I did not take home work to grade; it would be there when I got back. This was also helpfully reinforced when I had to get my daughter at daycare everyday by 4 p.m. What is a realistic boundary you can make here?

- How can you help prioritize your contract hours, and specifically your prep or planning periods? I would sometimes lock my door and turn most of the lights off during my prep. It helped me not to not get distracted by wayward students or a team member; I needed to use that time to get as much done as possible.

- Can you set up boundaries and utilize parent volunteers or student TAs for copies and help with overall classroom organization? How can you streamline this process? I was in a middle school that didn't have a PTA or parent volunteers but I could use a student TA. They became really helpful for making copies, organizing my classroom library, and general upkeeping of classroom supplies. Consider adding a section in your journal dedicated to your volunteer or TA to help you think about what they can take off your plate.

## Maintaining Healthy Relationships with Coworkers

As a teacher, you are likely working more than forty hours a week with your colleagues and—as a person that spent many years in a toxic work environment—building relationships with your team isn't just a good idea; it is vital to maintaining better mental health. I am not the best at fostering relationships. Instead, it is something I have to continually think about. What are some pieces you can focus on? Go through the following questions and think about how you might be able to create some goals or actionable items based on your answers.

- How often do you acknowledge and celebrate your coworkers' success? When someone is doing well on the team, everyone does well, so how can you take some time to make this a part of your weekly or monthly practice?

- How do the people on your team like to communicate? Make a list of your team members and write down how you can best get in contact with them. Some might like email or text messages, while others might prefer you to pop into their room for a quick chat. Knowing these preferences could cut back on your time waiting for a response, as well as help you better plan times to meet with them if they need the face-to-face connection.

- Are you a person that might not be a good listener? When collaborating with teammates, being an active listener helps you engage with your coworkers and build trust. I know there are times when I am trying really hard not to talk too much in a meeting, or to take leadership control. Participating in active listening strategies is an area in which I can always improve. Are you the person that might be talking too much in a collaboration meeting? Or are you a person that is maybe too quiet? Where do you fall in this spectrum? Build a spread in your journal where you tally in a meeting how much you talk compared to others. Or if you are the opposite and need to speak up more, tally how many times you have an opinion on something but choose not to speak up. Actively listening requires that you not only be present in the conversation and listen, but also that you respond to your teammates and build on their ideas.

- Go through some of these active listening question starters and write down the ones you like, then see if you can work one or two into a meeting in the coming weeks.

  - ◆ I'm picking up that...

  - ◆ As I understand it, you're saying...

  - ◆ What I guess I'm hearing is...

  - ◆ I'm not sure I'm with you, but...

  - ◆ Tell me more about how you see this...

  - ◆ If I were to do this lesson over again I would...

The most important thing with actively listening is to look for the main ideas in the conversation, try to avoid getting too distracted by the details, and focus on the key issues.

 # Chapter 5 Key Points

- If we can reimagine the art of doodling and see the inherent benefits (lower stress levels, higher sense of self, increased information retention), then we are more likely to doodle for ourselves as well as encourage it with our students. Your journal is a great place to practice the art of doodling.

- While studies show that daily gratitude can be beneficial, there is a fine line between daily gratitude and searching for something that might not be there. You can simply make note of the day in general rather than searching for positivity that might not be there. Trying a concept like a line a day in your journal can show you how to better understand this practice.

- Journaling is a great practice for people with neurodivergent minds. There are specific strategies that can be helpful, like starting simple or personalizing your use of the journal to create positive ownership of the process and object permanence so that it gets used and doesn't go missing.

- Dive deep into your own mental load, thinking from a perspective at home and at work, and think about ways to create a more equal social circle that is supportive, helpful, and allows you to have more time affluence.

# ISTE Standards Addressed

This chapter addresses several ISTE Standards, including

**2.1 Learner**

Educators continually improve their practice by learning from and with others and exploring proven and promising practices that leverage technology to improve student learning. Educators:

a. Set professional learning goals to explore and apply pedagogical approaches made possible by technology and reflect on their effectiveness.

**2.3 Empowering Leader**

Leaders create a culture where teachers and learners are empowered to use technology in innovative ways to enrich teaching and learning.

c. Inspire a culture of innovation and collaboration that allows the time and space to explore and experiment with digital tools.

 Reflection

After reading chapter 5, take some time to consider how you will apply some of the strategies to your own life and journal setup.

1. In the last chapter, we attempted some planner doodles, and you might have reflected on if they were something you could see yourself using in your journal. Now after reading about the mental benefits of doodling, has your opinion changed about adding this to your practice?

2. How do you define for yourself the fine line of having daily gratitude or searching for gratitude when it might not be there? What is a good amount of gratitude journaling for you?

3. What strategies did you find the most helpful for those with ADHD or autism? Do you have more ideas on how to help in this area? If you do, I would love to hear from you! DM me on Twitter **@MrsCarterHLA** or Instagram **@Nichole444**.

4. What invisible task challenges are you planning on trying? If you tried a few, which were the most helpful? Could you see yourself trying any of the coworker challenges with students? If so, how would the challenges need to be modified to work better for students working in groups?

# NOTES & DOODLES

# Conclusion

As this book comes to a close, I hope that you have taken steps toward creating a journal that works for you, unleashed your creativity, and become a little bit more productive. Keeping a journal for the past five years has been a source of hours of enjoyment for me. I love flipping back through all of my journals—at this point, I have a whopping fifteen of them. I remember all those times while I was growing up wishing that I could be a person that kept a diary, starting one and stopping, starting and stopping. This is what I always wanted to be able to do, and I am finally doing it. That is a huge personal accomplishment. Someone once said to me that these journals would be a wonderful legacy for my daughter to look back on one day, a little piece of her mom tucked away in these pages, and I just love that sentiment. My journals have become a place to write out my thoughts and feelings. In the last few years, I have gone through some of my highest highs professionally, and lowest lows personally, and when I look at the battered journals on my shelves, I recognize that.

As you keep going on your own journaling journey, know that there is so much inspiration out there for how to make this process work for you. I love using social media to inspire me when I am in a rut. Following creative journalers on Instagram is a great way to see other people's layouts and ideas. I also love watching people on YouTube plan a spread in their journal or set up their new one. (New journal setups usually come out on YouTube in January.) Pinterest is another space to go and find inspiration for layouts and themes. I love going to TikTok for journaling challenges, though Instagram has these, too. Scan the QR code to see a list of some of my favorite accounts to follow and tutorials to watch.

Social Media Follows

Another idea to keep your practice going is to build a journaling group. For a while, I had a group of four ladies that would come and do brunch at my house on a Sunday. We would bring out all our journaling pens, stickers, and washi tape and gossip together while we built our upcoming weekly pages. It buit community and was a great way to share and trade supplies. I have also helped set up a journaling club at a few schools, meeting before or after school, or during lunch. Students seem to really gravitate toward this idea—especially at the middle and high school levels—trading supplies and working in a communal space.

Just like with my other book on sketchnoting, when I saw this style of journaling, it spoke to me. I knew I wanted to try it out for myself, but I never imagined I would one day write a book on the topic for other teachers. I just knew it was something I loved doing and saw real tangible evidence that it was helping me be more creative and productive on a daily basis. I continue to consume content from people in the journaling community online and continue to practice and try new things. Remember, you can always start small and minimalistic as you find the style that works for you.

I would love to hear from you. Share your journal layouts and tag me in them on whatever social media platform you are on; using the hashtag **#TeacherJournaling**. If you see me at a conference, let's nerd out together with our journals. I am so excited you came with me on this journaling journey, and I hope you find joy and fun in creating in your journal, just like I have.

**Nichole**
 **@MrsCarterHLA**
**@Nichole444**

# References

Clear, J. (2018). *Atomic habits: An easy & proven way to build good habits & break bad ones.* New Yorkd, NY: Avery.

Finlay, Linda (2008). Reflecting on 'Reflective practice'. *Practice-based Professional Learning Paper 52,* The Open University.

Fisher, D.; Frey, N.; & Hattie, J. (2018). *Developing assessment capable learner*s. Thousand Oaks, CA: Corwin.

Hattie, J. (2008). *Visible Learning: A Synthesis of over 800 meta-analyses relating to achievement.* Oxfordshire, England, UK: Routledge.

Kleon, A. (2012). *Steal like an artist: 10 Things nobody told you about being creative.* New York, NY: Workman.

Morin, A. (2015) 7 Scientifically proven benefits of gratitude. *Psychology Today.* bit.ly/3N4CCOG

Otto, F. (2017). Making art activates brain's reward pathway – Drexel study. bit.ly/3KAFEss

Pillay, S. (2016). The "thinking" benefits of doodling. Harvard Health blog. bit.ly/3L55wfT

Smit, I. (2017). *A book that takes its time: An unhurried adventure in creative mindfulness (Flow).* New York, NY: Workman.

Whillans, A. (2020). *Time smart: How to reclaim your time & live a happier life.* Brighton, MA: Harvard Business Review Press.

# Index

## #

5 Dimensions of Teaching and
   Learning, 35
504 plans, 76, 129–130

## A

A Line A Day (gratitude journaling),
   121–123
ADHD and ADD, 3, 125–128
advisory periods, 42–43
Alexa (Amazon), 70–71
Arizona State University, 131, 134
Asana, 45
Atomic Habits, 48
autism, 129

## B

banners, 100
birthdays, 16, 73, 89
brain dump pages, 32
brainstorming, 32–33
breathing meditations, 33
Brown, Sunni, xi
Buddhism, 19
Bullet Journal Method, The, 36
bullet journaling®, 2–3, 21

## C

calendexes, 65
Calm (app), 13, 33
Canvas, 106, 126
Carroll, Ryder, 3, 36, 38
cell phones, 110
chunking, 38–39, 62
Citizen (ISTE standard), 21–22
ClassDojo, 126
Clear, James, 48
collages, 9–11
collection spreads, 32, 124
color coding, 59, 74–75
containers, 100
Cortana, 74–75
COVID-19 pandemic, 18, 61, 136
coworkers, 137–138
Cozi.com, 85
Creative Market, 113
creativity
   mental health and, 118–120
   productivity improving from, 6, 11, 21
   students and, 11, 128
   walking and, 13
Cricut, 111

# NOTES & DOODLES

# NOTES & DOODLES

# NOTES & DOODLES

# IF YOU LIKED THIS BOOK, CHECK OUT THESE GREAT ISTE TITLES!

*All books available in print and ebook formats at iste.org/books*

### Sketchnoting in the Classroom:
### A Practical Guide to Deepen Student Learning
BY NICHOLE CARTER

Author Nichole Carter shows how sketchnotes can help students retain new material, develop skills to articulate empathy and build connections to larger concepts. This book makes sketchnotes more accessible to all teachers and helps both teachers and students feel confident in visual note-taking.

iste.org/Sketchnoting

### Stretch Yourself:
### A Personalized Journey to Deepen Your Teaching Practice
BY CAITLIN MCLEMORE & FANNY PASSEPORT

Two award-winning young educators from opposite sides of the globe share their insights to guide teachers on how to take risks and innovate in their daily practice. Using the metaphor of yoga—with its focus on process and practice—the authors take teachers on a journey of self-reflection and assessment.

iste.org/StretchYourself

### Pathways to Well-Being:
### Helping Educators (and Others) Find Balance in a Connected World
BY SUSAN BROOKS-YOUNG & SARA ARMSTRONG

When we work toward supporting well-being for ourselves and others, our lives are enriched immensely. This insightful book offers practical examples and activities aimed at helping educators manage their technology use, so they can find balance in work and life.

iste.org/FindBalance

**LEARN AS A TEAM WITH ISTE BOOKS!**
ISTE's bulk books program makes team-based PD a breeze, and you'll save 35% or more off the retail price when you order large quantities. Email books@iste.org for details.

For exclusive discounts, giveaways and sneak previews of upcoming titles, sign up for the ISTE Books newsletter: iste.org/BooksNews

*ISTE members get 25% off every day!*